ALSO BY MAG...

The Busy Person's Guide To Energy Clearing

The Busy Person's Guide To Space Clearing

The Busy Person's Guide To Ghosts, Curses & Aliens

Caring For Your Animal Companion: The Intuitive, Natural Way To A Happy, Healthy Pet

Dowsing Ethics: Replacing Intentions With Integrity

The Practical Pendulum Series, Volumes 1-4

Pendulum Proficiency: You Can Learn To Dowse

How To Dowse Accurately & With Confidence

Dowsing Pitfalls & Protection

Dowse Your Way To Health: An Introduction To Health Dowsing

Dowsing: Practical Enlightenment

101 Amazing Things You Can Do With Dowsing

The Dowsing State

The Dowsing Encyclopedia

The Essence Of Dowsing by Nigel Percy

The Credibility Of Dowsing, edited by Nigel Percy

Healing Made Simple: Change Your Mind & Improve Your Health

Dowsing Box Set

Dowsing Reference Library

Visit Sixth Sense Books at www.sixthsensebooks.com to see a description of

all our books. We love writing about dowsing, healing, space clearing, intuitive pet care and energy work.

ASK THE RIGHT QUESTION

THE ESSENTIAL SOURCEBOOK OF GOOD DOWSING QUESTIONS

MAGGIE PERCY

NIGEL PERCY

Copyright © 2014 Sixth Sense Solutions

ISBN: 978-0-9978816-8-4 (Ebook version)

ISBN: 978-0-692-44455-9 (Paperback version)

All rights reserved. No part of this publication may be reproduced, distributed or transmitted in any form or by any means, including photocopying, recording, or other electronic or mechanical methods, without the prior written permission of the publisher, except in the case of brief quotations embodied in critical reviews and certain other noncommercial uses permitted by copyright law. For permission requests, write to the publisher, addressed "Attention: Permissions Coordinator," at the address below.

Sixth Sense Books

PO Box 617

Chino Valley, AZ 86323

www.sixthsensebooks.com

To All Members of the Dowsing Tribe: May You Enjoy The Journey

CONTENTS

PREFACE

Dowsing is a natural intuitive sensing ability all people have. Dowsing supercharges rational thought with instinctive reasoning. We like to think of it as focused intuition.

We developed the concept for this book after years of teaching dowsing courses and discussing dowsing at conferences and in online forums. It was obvious to us that many people were passionate about dowsing, but felt stuck at a low level of accuracy because they didn't know how to ask good dowsing questions. Most of them felt they lacked resources for taking their dowsing to the next level, whether the resource was time, money or a good teacher.

If you are interested in becoming an accurate dowser, this guide will help you. Our goal is to make it easier for you to dowse about things you are interested in, but haven't felt confident enough to dowse about. This book requires minimum effort, time and money. But you still need to invest in using it to get results.

Even if you have never taken a course, this book will help you. However, if you are new to dowsing, we suggest you study the dowsing lesson included in the Resources section to make sure your technique includes all the essentials.

It is quite likely you will discover that our dowsing lesson includes subjects you never learned about in any other course. Getting a solid grounding in the basics of dowsing technique is an important factor in accuracy.

You can use the material in this book in any order you wish. Some people will keep it handy as a reference guide of good dowsing questions. Others will use it as a 'workshop in a book' for honing their dowsing technique. The most dedicated will use it for both purposes.

If you have any of our other books on dowsing, this is different. We wrote this book in answer to a need we perceived among dowsers for having good, ready-made dowsing questions. People just didn't know what to ask, and we felt a book of good questions would be a big help. Then we decided to add some worksheets for those who wanted to learn to create good questions that would be more customized.

One of the biggest stumbling blocks in dowsing is learning to ask good questions. Once you've mastered this material, you will find your dowsing has improved significantly. But you won't see progress by putting this book on a shelf and ignoring it. So dig in and enjoy!

Maggie Percy

Chino Valley, AZ

July 19, 2014

USING THIS GUIDE

Introduction

CORRECT ANSWERS ARE Vital to Dowsers

Whether you've been dowsing for years or are just beginning, probably your biggest challenge is getting accurate answers when dowsing. If you're like most dowsers, you are keen on getting the answers to your questions. But then, when you get them, they appear to be wrong too often. So you mistrust your dowsing and don't use it much. You think maybe you don't have the talent of a Master Dowser.

If you think that, you're wrong. Anyone can learn to dowse well. But like any skill you have-musical or athletic ability are examples-your dowsing will improve with training and practice.

WHAT DOWSING ISN'T...

One of the biggest disservices done to dowsing is to lump it with 'psychic' abilities. People have the mistaken impression that you either have a full-blown psychic ability or not. So you may think you should be able to dowse accurately from the get-go. This misconception is stopping you from being the dowser you can be.

So What Exactly IS Dowsing?

Dowsing is the word used to describe the activity of using your intuitive sensing abilities in a focused way.

You are familiar with your physical senses, which gather information about the world around you using your eyes, ears, nose, skin and tongue. The information you gather about your physical environment using your physical senses allows you to make better choices. From simple decisions: "Don't touch that stove. It's hot." To bigger ones: "This food tastes spoiled, so I won't eat it." To even bigger ones: "That man has a gun. I'm going to run for cover."

In addition to your physical senses, you also have intuitive sensing abilities, but our culture has trained you not to believe in them or to mistrust them. Often called 'intuition', your intuitive senses are cast as unreliable or even freaky, simply because they work differently than your physical senses. The instant information provided by your physical senses can be 'rationalized', but the intuitive hits you get, which come just as fast and equally out of 'nowhere', somehow seem odd.

But almost everyone has experienced getting information from their intuitive senses. Examples are: knowing someone is going to call right before they do; not feeling right about doing something, though you aren't sure why; just 'knowing' that something is the right choice, even though you have no data to prove it.

Intuition is a vital part of your life, as it can give you useful information without you having to go through a linear, fact-gathering and analysis process, which can take a lot of time. Intuition is particularly helpful in crisis situations, and no doubt served our ancestors well when there were many dangers in their environment.

Intuitive hits may come often or rarely, but they are not the result of you choosing to use your intuitive senses. Dowsing is a method of **focusing** your intuitive sensing abilities to gather information, much the same way that looking in a focused way at a scene helps you collect visual data that casually glancing at it won't.

By learning to dowse well, you will hone your intuitive sensing abilities, allowing you to gather much more of the useful information you need to make healthy, successful choices in life.

Another way of looking at dowsing is to say it is a 'whole brain' activity. Our culture emphasizes the power of the left (or rational) part of the brain. But you have a right brain, too. It is creative, intuitive and is the perfect partner to your linear, logical left brain. Yet most people ignore the right brain.

Dowsers use the left brain to create a good dowsing question and the right brain to access the answer. This balances and strengthens the function of your brain, using it as it was designed to be used. Why use only half of your brain when you can use all of it?

Learn To Dowse

Please take our free dowsing lesson before using this book. Most people don't have adequate training, and taking our lesson will bring you up to speed on the basics. See the Resources section for a link to our free video and written lessons.

What The Heck Are Scales?

Throughout this book, you will see references to answers that are more complex than simple yes/no answers. Scales help you get a degree of 'yes' and 'no' that really gives you more useful information when dowsing. If you have never dowsed using scales, please see the Appendix for instructions of how to use scales in dowsing.

. . .

Don't Make Excuses...You Can Do This!

All the Master Dowsers you have heard about started out where you are now. They didn't spring from the womb with a pendulum in hand. They aren't 100% accurate. But through years of experience and learning, they have honed their dowsing skills and have become amazingly accurate. You can do the same, and we want to make that journey fun and easy for you.

This book is filled with practical techniques and ready-made dowsing questions that will help improve your dowsing accuracy. If you aren't confident or don't feel you have time to study how to make your own dowsing questions, you can use the ones we've created.

While this book is aimed at covering the subject of how to ask a dowsing question comprehensively, it is not a dowsing training overall. We have included a link to a free, complete lesson in the Resources section and urge you to peruse that before starting, as even asking good questions won't work if your basic technique is faulty.

You can use this book to take your dowsing to the next level and beyond. It's totally up to you how far you go, but if you keep growing as a dowser, one day you'll find that you are a Master Dowser.

We Look Forward to Helping You!

We want to help you see how dowsing can improve your life, but to do that, you need to be a more accurate and confident dowser. If you are accurate, you will dowse more. If you dowse more, you can dowse about more things. And pretty soon, you'll find, like us, that dowsing totally transforms your life.

∾

Disclaimer, Warning & What To Expect

How Fast Will You Master Dowsing?

Dowsing is a natural ability we all have. But that doesn't mean you can pick up a pendulum and immediately be a great dowser.

The best athletes spend many hours training with coaches who have impressive credentials. So too, if you want to be able to dowse like a master, you will need to study, learn and practice like we have.

We believe anyone can learn to dowse well. But we want to be honest with you. It took years of dowsing many times a day about lots of subjects for us to become this good at it.

This Book is the Real Deal

So if you are just treating dowsing like some kids treat ouija boards, this book is not for you. Dowsing can be used as a party trick or hobby, but this book is for people who want to benefit from their dowsing beyond its entertainment value. In other words, this book is for serious dowsers. And that means you will need to devote some time in order to reap the full benefits.

Don't Expect Miracles...But Expect Progress

Be realistic in your expectations. Dowsing is not 100% accurate. Nothing is. You don't always get the right answers using your left brain, and you won't always get the right answers using dowsing. But overall, we have found that dowsing increases our accuracy when making choices, and that's a reasonable goal to have.

Dowsing is potentially one of the most empowering techniques you will ever encounter. That means you can take control of your life and get better results than you've been getting. But the flip side of that is you also must take responsibility for the choices you make. Dowsing puts you in the driver's seat. Where you end up is up to you.

ETHICS MATTER

Because dowsing is so powerful, it is important to use it only when appropriate. It is unethical to dowse for or about others who have not asked you to do so. And it is just silly to dowse about things that you are not properly trained to dowse about. Don't dowse life or death questions unless you believe you are up to the task, and even then, get a second and third opinion before taking action.

DOWSING IS NOT a Substitute for Your Doctor

Last but not least, the material in this book is not designed to diagnose or prescribe for you. Please see your health care professional if you have any health issues. But you have the right to learn to use your intuition and dowsing and educational background to make informed choices in your own health care, and for your children and pets. Dowsing can be a valuable tool in that respect, but only if you learn to use it responsibly, ethically and with appropriate training. Please dowse responsibly!

THE QUESTION IS MORE IMPORTANT THAN THE ANSWER

Take Your Time!

GRABBING your pendulum and dowsing without thinking is a sure way to get a wrong or confusing answer. We've all done it, especially when we were new to dowsing. But those of us who persevered and tried to figure out why our answers were wrong were rewarded. We soon discovered that asking a good question is one of the keys to being a Master Dowser.

If you are in a hurry or don't want to spend time learning how to create great dowsing questions right now, you can skip to the chapters with ready-made questions. But sooner or later, you may want to dive deeper into dowsing, so we're providing additional material that will help boost your learning curve in dowsing by shortcutting the trial and error method we had to use.

This chapter covers the basics in how to create a Master Dowser quality dowsing question. In subsequent chapters, we have added worksheets to help you use these principles to create specialized questions on key dowsing topics.

Use Your Whole Brain

WE MAY SOUND PRETTY perfectionistic about making 'good' dowsing questions, but the truth is, most people don't dowse a lot, even if they want to, because they don't trust their dowsing. Their answers are not accurate, so they quit dowsing.

We believe that one of the key things you can do to become an accurate, confident dowser is to ask clear dowsing questions. Then, you will get good answers. And you will begin to trust and use your dowsing. To do that, you use both sides of the brain.

WHOLE BRAIN DOWSING

The left part of your brain has different functions from the right half. Your left brain is rational and logical, and it likes to address things in sequence. Your right brain is more creative, intuitive and leaps about when thinking.

Everyone has a preference for using one side of their brain. Mathematicians, engineers and scientists tend to prefer the left brain (although really innovative ones use the right brain a lot). Artists, musicians and intuitives prefer to use the right brain.

So who is right? There is no right or wrong choice. Your preference is just a preference, determined by your natural talents and the culture you grew up in, which rewarded you for certain types of behavior.

But here is the undeniable truth: you have two parts to your brain for a very good reason. If you use both appropriately, you will have a happier, healthier, more successful life. The trick is learning when to rely on which side.

Dowsing is the only intuitive method we know of that uses both sides of the brain in a balanced way. Because of that, dowsing helps you become a more balanced person--if you do it right-- and that leads to an overall better life, because you aren't always trying to deal with things with only half a brain. (There's a joke in there somewhere...)

Many right brain dominant individuals prefer to grab a pendulum and begin to dowse without thinking too much about a question (of course). This is because forming a question is a left brain activity, and they feel weak at that. This book is designed to give you good, left brain-designed questions so that you can learn how it feels to use both sides of your brain when dowsing. It will also give you much greater accuracy.

If you are left brain dominant, this book will make a lot of sense to you and save you a lot of time and effort, but you may have to focus on letting the left brain take a break when you actually begin to dowse. In other words, tell your rational mind to shut up and sit down so the right brain can do its thing. This can be pretty challenging, as left brain dominant individuals like to have the left brain in charge all the time. Well, that doesn't work in dowsing.

To become a good dowser, you will be challenged to use parts of your brain you don't often use. That is part of the personal growth dowsing offers, and it can transform your life in beautiful ways. But let's get back to the idea of dowsing questions and what makes a good one.

BAD DOWSING QUESTIONS

To better understand good dowsing questions, let's first examine what makes a question 'bad'. Bad dowsing questions often have some things in common. Of course, they give 'wrong' answers. But how can you spot a bad question? Here are some general rules:

- Bad dowsing questions are very short
- Bad dowsing questions use vague words like 'good', 'healthy' and 'highest and greatest good'
- Bad dowsing questions are quickly created

- Bad dowsing questions are based on emotion and you often have emotional attachment to a particular answer
- Bad dowsing questions are asked without thinking about what your goal is, what you mean by the words, or how you will measure the success of the answer
- Bad dowsing questions usually are used (often unintentionally) for the purpose of confirming an answer you already think you know, or an opinion you want to bolster.

In short, bad dowsing questions lack appropriate left brain input. The left brain is the logical, rational part of your mind. It is well-suited to helping you create a good dowsing question.

Unfortunately, many dowsers fail to check in with their left brain when dowsing. This may be because they don't feel that is a strength they have, or they haven't practiced doing it. Or perhaps they feel that using their left brain is a denial of their heart. Sometimes it's just natural laziness, and other times, it's fear of hearing the 'truth'.

We have found that the best results in dowsing (and in life) come from a balanced approach. You have a left brain and a right brain for a reason. You have a brain and a heart for a reason. Using both appropriately will give you far better results than using only one.

Since creating good dowsing questions is largely a left brain activity, this book will be about helping you to use your rational faculties well. (Actual dowsing uses your right brain, and we won't be spending a lot of time on that in this book. You can check out our other books and courses if you feel you need help with your intuition or heart.)

Description Of A Good Dowsing Question

Aspects of a Good Dowsing Question

A good dowsing question is specific, detailed and uses clearly defined terms. Throughout this book, we will be reinforcing how you can apply these principles.

Specific: A good dowsing question asks about one thing. It is not effective or efficient to bundle questions together. It's just confusing. Ask one question about each particular subject.

Example: You are eager to become more healthy, and you aren't trained in biology or medicine, so you aren't too sure what terms to use. You want to feel energetic, be strong and not get sick. Plus you want to get rid of that pain in your joints.

You may be tempted to try and bundle it all together and ask what supplement or therapy will be 'best' for your 'health', but that will not give accurate results. You will need to make a question for each goal.

Detailed: A good dowsing question will address who, what, where, when, how and why as appropriate. Each of those things may require a specific word or phrase. That means that a good dowsing question is usually long.

Example: You want a supplement that will strengthen your immune system, because you don't want to get the flu. You may be tempted to ask, "Will this supplement help me avoid the flu?" or "Is this the best supplement for my immune system?"

Neither of those questions is detailed enough. Instead, you want to consider all important aspects that will give you the results you desire. So instead, you may ask, "Is _____(specific supplement) an 8 or better on a scale of 10, where 10 is the best results for strengthening my immune system so I can avoid the flu, without side effects, when taken as directed for at least 30 days at this time?" If price is important, you need to factor that into the question, perhaps by adding the phrase, "...without side effects and for the best price for my budget..."

As you can see, the question will be long. You can write it down, read it a few times, then point at it while dowsing, saying, "Is the answer to this question a yes?" or "What is the answer to this question?"(when using a scale). That way you don't have to remember it.

Clearly defined terms: Too often, we see dowsers use vague terms like 'good', 'healthy' or 'highest good'. Sometimes, they use terms other people have taught them to use, but they haven't thought exactly what those terms mean.

You need to be very clear about the words you use when dowsing. You need to think about what exactly they mean to you, not to the guru who taught you. Spend time looking at your dowsing question and ask yourself how you define each term. Ask yourself if you can be more specific. Instead of 'good', define what you mean. That wine may be 'good' for you if you mean tastes good, but it may not be good for you if you mean no sulfites or additives.

You can use the dictionary definition of a term if you like. Or you can define it for yourself. Or you can use someone else's definition. But be aware that **each one may give a different answer**.

You also need to be aware that your subconscious may have a different definition than you consciously have, which can lead to mistakes. Our subconscious is tasked with keeping us safe, and many of the things you will dowse about could touch a raw nerve with your subconscious.

Your subconscious has many faulty beliefs about love, health, wealth, success and happiness. When you become a spiritual seeker, and you begin to try to transform your life, you may become very frustrated, because your subconscious does not want you to change.

It can be amusing or scary to see what your subconscious believes about important subjects, and that alone is a wonderful exercise in transformational dowsing. Dowsing is the easiest, most effective way of finding out what your subconscious believes and then finding the best way to align it with your conscious goals.

This topic will be touched on later in this book, but deserves an entire workshop or book of its own, as it is so important. (While we will give sample dowsing questions, this book is not about clearing or healing techniques, so those won't be covered.)

ASKING the Question

Once you have created your dowsing question, there are some steps you can follow that may help make your dowsing process easier and more accurate.

1. Write your question down. That way, you don't have to remember every word, plus it makes it easy to go back and check it later.
2. Read your question a few times. See if you feel you have covered all the aspects that matter to you. Change as needed.
3. Read the final question several times, focusing on it intently.
4. Get into a dowsing state and dowse the answer by saying, "What is the answer to this question?" (That way you don't have to remember the question.)

CONFIRMING the Answer

Once you have your answer, write it down. When you have results, go back and look at your question.

If you feel the answer was correct, then try to duplicate the process next time you dowse. If the answer appeared to be wrong, take the time to try and figure out how it could have been right.

Example: We applied for a home loan modification. After 18+ months of sending in paperwork, we were turned down. I had consistently dowsed we would get a loan modification.

More than three years later, our mortgage was sold to another company. That company asked if we'd like to apply for a home loan. I was suspicious, but went ahead. We got the loan modification easily and quickly.

Turned out that when I had dowsed the question, I had not put a time in it. I just asked would we get a modification on our loan. The answer appeared to be wrong, but it was correct. We did eventually get the modification- 3 yrs later.

If I had asked, "Will we get THIS particular home loan modification?", I would have probably gotten the correct answer. Lesson learned.

Your 'wrong' dowsing answers can teach you more about dowsing than your 'right' answers if you use them well.

DOWSING QUESTIONS ON FAVORITE TOPICS

What Can You Use Dowsing For?

OVER THE YEARS, we have met and spoken with many people who have used dowsing. In that time we found that there were several major areas which were of interest to them. These key topics are what we have concentrated on here.

The chapters that follow contain the most useful questions that cover these key topics: health, wealth, relationships, career and major life choices. Please study the dowsing lesson in the Resources before using the questions. If you are not in a proper dowsing state, you won't get correct answers even with these questions. If you are not an ethical dowser, you probably won't get satisfying answers.

Dowsing is about using both sides of your brain, the rational and intuitive, in a focused way to get answers to questions you couldn't answer using just your rational mind. So dowsing is about getting answers. That's all.

Dowsing is not a healing or energy transforming technique. If someone has taught you that, they are mistaken. Dowsing is about getting answers; about gathering information. Then you can use whatever method you like to clear or transform energy or to heal.

The problem with some dowsing gurus is that they are teaching that you can swing a pendulum and change someone or something or some situation. What they really mean is they advocate using intention to create change.

We believe intention is ALWAYS what creates change, no matter what method you are using. But we have two warnings. The first concern is that most people do not have powerful and focused enough energy to change things simply using a statement of intent. What happens is their desire becomes a 'wish'. Rarely does that change anything. So if you want to get the great results gurus get with intention, you need to work on your own energy field and become a powerful conscious manifester. That doesn't happen overnight.

Our second concern is that dowsing is not about intention, though it goes well with intention. Just swinging a pendulum does NOT change things. That is a misconception. We find that most people get better results when clearing or healing or balancing energies if they anchor their intention using a specific method. Choose one that works for you.

We aren't sure how this misconception started. It may have been because of a burning desire to show how great dowsing is, and what could be better than having it change or heal things as easily as if your pendulum is a magic wand? Healing methods are very popular, and there was a temptation to call dowsing a healing method. However, in our opinion, not only is that a misnomer, but it does dowsing a grave disservice. Dowsing supports and extends the results when used alongside any healing method, but it isn't just for health questions.

NOTE:

In the chapters that follow, you will find dowsing questions to cover most of the key issues you are interested in. At the end of each chapter, the dowsing questions may be found in a chart with blank columns.

There are two copies in case you forget to make a copy of the blank chart.

The charts are useful in tracking your progress over time. Often, you will want to dowse the same questions at certain intervals: daily, weekly or monthly. These blank charts can be filled with your dowsing answers and each column dated so you can track your results.

HEALTH DOWSING QUESTIONS

Overview

You Are Responsible For Your Health

People generally don't like that word 'responsible', because they think it means 'blame', as in, "It's your fault you have that illness or symptom." Responsibility doesn't mean blame when used this way. It's about taking control of your health and being the one who determines outcomes. People too often give their power away to a doctor or cultural belief without even thinking what it means to them.

The person who cares most about your health should be you. That means YOU need to become conscious and take an active role in your healing process. While it is excellent to get good advice and support, it is not healthy in the long run to let someone else have total control of your health process. Don't expect anyone to care more about your health than you do.

Always Get A Second (And Third) Opinion

No one knows it all. Especially in important health situations, always seek a second or third opinion. And count your opinion as paramount. It's wise to get opinions from people with different perspectives; otherwise, you just hear the same thing over and over. Interestingly, when health crises occur, that's when we see people consulting outside the allopathic professional community, as they instinctively realize that to get another opinion, you have to ask people with a different perspective. Sometimes a health crisis therefore becomes a great opportunity for you to see health in new ways.

FIND A HEALTH Care Professional You Trust And Work With Her (Him)

You need help in your healing process. Dowsing can really be a great resource, but you also need professional advice. Pick a professional who respects your opinions and listens to you. It is especially helpful to find someone who is open to how you perceive things and will support you. There are caring professionals out there, so don't get hung up with someone who puts you down and acts like a dictator.

BE An Active Partner In Creating The Health You Want

Don't keep your mouth shut around your doctor. Speak up and participate in the process. This is your health, and what you think matters. You will find it easier to create the health you want if you see yourself as empowered.

USING The Questions In This Chapter

This chapter is divided into a number of subjects that we have found are of common interest to dowsers. Questions will be listed along with the goals you have for asking them. For those who want to create their own question, notes are added that will give you tips on how to customize dowsing questions on that subject.

Evaluating Your Blocks To Health

OVERALL HEALTH

A good place to start when health dowsing is to get an overall picture of how your physical body is doing; where it is strong and where it could use some assistance to become stronger. You can dowse the answers to whichever questions you want, and then look at the results to get a picture of your overall physical health.

On a scale of +10 to -10, with 0 being average for my gender, age and culture, what is my overall physical health at this time?

Obviously, a 0 is average; minus numbers are less than average; plus numbers are better than average.

SYSTEM HEALTH

You can test the physical health of various organs and systems using the same type of question by substituting the following one by one in the blank:

(You may look these up online to get more complete definitions)

Nervous System: central nervous system (brain) and nerves

Circulatory System: heart, arteries, veins

Reproductive System: ovaries, uterus, testes

Endocrine System: glands like thyroid, adrenals

Digestive System: stomach, intestines, mouth

Urinary System: bladder

Skeletal System: bones, ligaments, tendons, cartilage

Respiratory System: lungs

Muscle System: muscles, sometimes includes the heart

Integumentary System: (hair, skin, nails)

Lymphatic system

On a scale of +10 to -10, with 0 being average for my gender, age and culture, what is the overall physical health of my _____ System at this time?

Write the answers down and get a picture of how your overall health is doing in each area.

ORGAN HEALTH

You can then dig deeper and see which part of a particular system is weakest. Using a search engine or book, list the organs and parts of each system. Let's use the Digestive System as an example:

The parts of the Digestive System are:

salivary glands,

esophagus,

stomach,

liver,

gall bladder,

pancreas,

intestines,

rectum,

anus.

Let's say you got a lower number than you would like for the physical health of your digestive system. Your next step is to find out where you need to focus your effort in healing and balancing it.

So you ask the same question again, this time substituting, one at a time, the different parts of the digestive system. Write the answers down.

On a scale of +10 to -10, with 0 being average for my gender, age and culture, what is the overall physical health of my _____ at this time?

When To Take Action On The Above

In general, we would regard -8 or worse to be a number that would cause us to want to take action right away to balance and heal the system (if we found that another dowser agreed with our answers, or a doctor's test agreed). If you are in the low minus numbers, you can take gentle action. You can even work to improve your rating if you got above 0. Obviously, an 8 or above is a terrific place to be.

Check out Dowsing Supplements, Remedies and Therapies and When To Consult a Professional if you need to do some work on some part of your body.

Key Subjects To Test

There are some processes or situations that can affect health that don't always reside in a single system or organ, yet they can contribute to or indicate a major health imbalance. These aspects are:

toxicity,

inflammation,

infection,

trauma,

cancer,

parasites.

Test for each subject by substituting one by one in the question below, and write your answers down.

On a scale of 0 to 10, with 0 being none and 10 being the worst/most it could be, what is the level/degree of physical_____ in my physical body at this time?

The reason we ask about 'physical' toxicity, inflammation, etc. Is that you can have energetic issues, and they require different treatment. So you can test the level of energetic toxicity, inflammation, etc. separately.

INTERPRETING Results On The Previous Question

We have found that 0-3 is fairly common for most of the subjects in the previous question, though 0 is of course the best answer to get. At 3, one tends to start seeing physical symptoms. At 8, whatever is causing the problem really needs attention, usually by a professional.

Aura & Chakras

Aura

It will be useful to take a course or at least read a good book about the aura to understand it better. Barbara Brennan's book "Hands of Light" is very helpful in this regard. However, it is also very detailed, and so this chapter will present a much more abbreviated version of dowsing the health of the aura which will allow even beginners to use dowsing to check the health of their auras. Those who want to dive deeper should get Barbara's book.

The aura has layers. The seven layers operate on different planes, with three of them on the physical plane. You can have problems at any level, and the problems can be many different types. However, for the purposes of this book, we won't get into which layer is affected, but instead will do an overall evaluation to find problems and resolve them.

What is the overall health of my aura at this time, on a scale of 0 to 10, with 10 being optimal health for me?

An 8 or above is considered a very good score. Lower means that there is probably something going on that is affecting the integrity of the aura. Using a book or other resource, make a list of the potential problems you can have with your aura. Examples could be:

tear,

burn,

infection,

block.

You can substitute mechanisms into the following question one by one to find out what the problem is (and remember there may be more than one):

Are there any _____ at this time in my aura that are having a significant effect on the health and well-being of my aura?

If you get yes, you can then go to remedies/therapies and find out what will help resolve the issue.

Chakras

Your body has many minor chakras, but 7 major ones. Problems with the chakras can lead to physical ailments. "Hands of Light" is a very good book that covers dowsing the chakras in detail. We won't go into that depth here. Instead, this is a good starting point for evaluating your chakra function using dowsing.

There are two obvious ways to dowse your chakras. Maggie was introduced to dowsing through her Karuna Reiki Master Teacher class, where the instructor pulled out a pendulum and showed that the movement of the pendulum, when held over the chakras, gave information about how that chakra was functioning. In Barbara Brennan's book, she details the types of pendulum movements. So if you are interested in taking it further, definitely refer to her book.

For the purposes of this book, we will simplify the process so you can begin to get useful information about the functioning of the chakras. There are a few basic pendulum movements you will see when you evaluate the chakra:

1) Circular (in either direction)

2) Linear (in various directions/angles)

3) No movement at all

4) A complex daisy-like series of 'flower petal' circles (in either direction)

If you are evaluating someone else's chakras, you can have them lie on their back while you hold the pendulum over each chakra, asking to see the function. If you are evaluating your own chakras or working long distance with someone, you can just ask to see the function of whatever chakra. In either case, you start the pendulum in a neutral swing or circle, then ask to see how that chakra is working.

Be patient and allow the pendulum to settle into whatever movement is appropriate. It may even need to reverse direction, so make sure you give it a good swing to start, so it has plenty of motion to work with.

Here is a very simplified summary of what the different pendulum motions mean:

1) Circular: normal, size of circle showing how much energy flowing or how open

2) Linear: lines indicate there is some kind of block to normal function

3) No movement means the chakra is shut down

4) A daisy shape indicates a lot of transformational energy is present

A nice, big circle is usually a 'good' thing. The daisy shape shows a person is changing, which is neither good nor bad, but depends on various factors. Linear usually means some work would be advisable. A shut down chakra can lead to illness, pain and other negative consequences, so it is wise to address it immediately.

You can use dowsing to get further information about causes of problems and to choose the best way to remedy dysfunction.

EM Field

YOUR BODY'S ELECTROMAGNETIC FIELD, which relates to the activity of your brain and heart, has a huge but little-known impact on your health, well-being and ability to manifest your desires. Dowsing is an excellent tool for evaluating your EM Field; the causes of problems; and how to strengthen it.

Michele Fitzgerald of the Senzar Learning Center is the one who pioneered the work on the EM Field and how it relates to various aspects of your life back in 2009. It is beyond the scope of this book to go into full detail about the EM Field, so if you want to dive deeper into this important subject, you will want to consult the Resources section for a link to Michele's website.

Note: The EM Field is not your aura, nor does it have anything to do with EMFs (electromagnetic fields). It is generated by the activity of the brain and heart, and it is electromagnetic in origin. A stronger EM

Field gives you greater protection of all kinds and helps you manifest positive outcomes more easily. You feel good and have a higher energy level when your EM Field is strong.

Sadly, our research shows that most people have an EM Field operating at less than 35%. In most cases, much less. You don't have to be a dowser to know when your EM Field is low. You feel exhausted and unmotivated and struggle to just do what needs doing.

The EM Field is actually rather easy to bring into the 30% range in most cases, and that will give you a real boost of energy and motivation. We have found color therapy seems to work well on most people for strengthening a weak EM Field.

EVALUATE YOUR EM Field

On a scale of 0 to 100%, with 100% being the best and most optimal functioning, what is the value of my EM Field as an average over the last 7 days?

Note that you can dowse several times for several different time periods to get a feel for how your EM Field has been operating over time. Instead of the 7 day average, you can test the 30 day / 60 day / 1 year averages.

Generally we test a 7 day average, because even thinking about testing it and wanting it to be a higher value will actually raise the level temporarily. The EM Field value varies over a +10% to -10% range over the course of a given day. So if you got 30% (which most people won't), then your EM Field probably has been between 20-40% over that time period.

CAUSES OF EM Field Issues

There are actually many variables that can cause your EM Field to crash or be very low. Some have to do with poor boundaries and beliefs allowing others' energies to affect you. Some have to do with external electromagnetic fields we all are exposed to, like wifi and other EMFs. If you are interested in learning more about the EM Field and what can affect it, check into Michele Fitzgerald's trainings through the link in the Resources section.

Repairing The EM Field

Most people will find they are below 30% when they dowse their EM Field value. We have found color therapy to be the easiest way to repair the EM Field. The most common colors that dowse as appropriate are: red, blue, purple, silver and gold.

Dowse which color or colors are best to help repair, restore and strengthen your EM Field, if it is below 35%.

Is red/blue/purple/silver/gold the best color for me to use to repair, restore and strengthen my EM Field at this time? (Dowse about each color individually.)

Sometimes two colors do better than one. So after you get the first color, ask:

Is using two colors better than using one for me to repair, restore and strengthen my EM Field at this time?

If you get 'yes', then test and find which color is the second color you need to use.

Once you have the color(s) you need, then wear it, look at it or carry it with intention. When wearing it, that means wear that color clothing (it doesn't have to be a large item or on the surface; you can carry a scrap of material that color or wear socks that color). To look at it, choose an item in your environment that is the right color and stare at the color for 60-90 seconds twice a day with intention. To carry the color, use a crayon or colored pencil to color a piece of paper, and put it in your pocket or shoe, wearing it with intention.

Here is the intention to use:

"Please repair, restore and strengthen my EM Field to its highest appropriate level at this time."

How long do you do this? Do it until your EM Field tests at least in the 30s and you feel much better. How long will that take? In most cases, less than two weeks. Sometimes one or two days.

If you are unable to get your field at least into the 30s by doing color therapy, you probably have an unusual mechanism affecting you, and you could benefit from getting professional help to discover the cause and resolve it. We suggest you take Michele's course if this happens, because there are very few professionals aware of the EM Field and how to repair it.

∾

Supplements & Remedies

DOWSING for supplements is perhaps one of the most common practical applications of dowsing. Yet most people do not dowse their supplements in such a way that they reap the most benefits they can. In this section, we will help show you how you can use dowsing to evaluate supplements, side effects, how long it will take to see results and how your entire supplement program is working for you. We'll also give you some valuable tips on supplement dowsing that will save you a lot of money and give you better results.

Remember that supplements work slowly. It can take up to 120 days for them to give results, unless your system is really deficient, in which case you may see quick results. So when you find something, give it a fair chance to work.

Note: You can use all these same questions to test the usefulness of herbal and homeopathic remedies, flower essences and essential oils for helping you achieve goals with symptoms and conditions.

• • •

Is A Supplement Or Remedy What You Need?

There's a lot of controversy, and always has been, about supplements and their usefulness. In a sense everyone is correct. Supplements are useless if they are poor quality. Don't waste money on cheap supplements. Supplements are NOT a substitute for a good diet. Research and find the best, healthiest diet you can, and you won't need as many supplements.

Your body is changing constantly, and its need for various minerals and vitamins changes over time. So any single supplement or program probably is not going to be the lifetime solution for you. And finally, good supplements are expensive, but you take supplements to achieve excellent health. If they work, you won't be sick; you won't have degenerative disease; you'll live a more active, healthy life. What's that worth to you?

For general supplementation, as in creating a balance of minerals and vitamins for optimal physical function, use the following question while testing bottles on a shelf in the health food store, or the products in a catalog or on a website:

Will supplementation by any of these products be an 8 or higher on a scale of 10 (with 10 being the most helpful) for creating excellent immune balance, good energy levels and excellent physical function for my body at this time when taken as directed?

If you get 'no', then it's probably not worth supplementing at this time. If you get 'yes', then you need to find which one or ones to buy. Think about your key requirements and needs for a 'yes' answer: price, side effects, allergic reaction, digestibility, absorbability, how quickly they act, how effective they are, etc. Everyone has different requirements, so put all yours together and say a 10 is a product that fulfills all of them to your satisfaction.

Next, be very clear about why you want to take supplements. What is excellent health to you? High energy levels? Good digestion? Feeling pain free? Staying healthy instead of catching colds? Etc. Don't expect to get a good answer if you are unclear about how you define health.

Are any of these products an 8 or higher on a scale of 10 for reaching my overall health goals at this time when taken as directed?

If you get a lot of possible products, trim the list down by asking if any are a 10 on a scale of 10, then dowse among them. If you don't get any that are 8 or better, go to another website, store or provider and test their products. Don't waste money on anything that is less than an 8 as a rule.

Ideally you want to get down to one product that is a 10 and then give it a try. If you are particularly deficient, this may not be possible. If you have a large overall deficiency, our advice is to get on an excellent combination vitamin/mineral supplement instead of treating symptoms. Most of your symptoms will often disappear if you balance your system with a good overall supplement that covers all the bases. Then you can address any lingering issues, which should be far fewer. Give the plan 90-120 days to work. Remember to see a doctor if your symptoms are serious.

FACTORS TO CONSIDER **When Dowsing Supplements And Remedies**

Your digestion is a huge factor in the effectiveness of your supplements. You must absorb something for it to work. If your digestive system is inflamed or you have food allergies or leaky gut, you may not get the results promised. If you know you have a digestive challenge, spend time healing your gut. There are many natural ways to do this, and it is worth the effort.

Supplementation ideally should be a short term phenomenon. By short term, we mean not your whole life. It is best to get your nutrients from your diet. However, even a good organic diet with lots of fruits and veggies often won't provide enough minerals, due to the sorely depleted state of soils. Minerals are critical for bodily function, and your dowsing will help you determine when you need additional ones.

Anything can be an allergen. Even something 'good'. Be sure to test for whether you have any allergic or sensitivity reaction to a given supplement or any ingredient in it (there are a shocking number of 'extra' ingredients) before buying it. See the later section on this topic.

It's generally unwise to supplement only one mineral, like calcium. That's because so many minerals work in conjunction with others, and when you raise the value of one, you may inadvertently create an imbalance with another. Magnesium, for example, is closely tied to calcium. Potassium depends on magnesium. And so on. You want an optimal balance in your body of all minerals. So unless you have been diagnosed with a mineral deficiency, don't load one mineral, or you may just create another deficiency.

It's best to work with a health care professional to determine the best overall strategy of supplementation for your needs. If that professional wants to recommend their own brand of product, you can then elect to dowse and see if their suggestion is an 8 or better for your goals.

How Long To Take It?

Be patient about results. But don't think you'll need to supplement forever. You can dowse what the optimal time length to take the chosen supplement will be.

How long would it be best for me to take this supplement to reach my health goals:

More than 30 days?

More than 60 days?

More than 90 days?

Just change the question until you get the time frame that says 'yes'.

An alternative question that is just as good, once you pick a particular supplement, would be:

How many bottles of this supplement taken at the suggested dosage will be required for me to reach my health goals?

1?

2?

3?

If you are not happy with how large the numbers/time get, then feel free to check and see if another product from another store or catalog can do better overall for you.

EVALUATING Results

Assuming you marked the calendar for how long it would take to get results, when that date arrives, you want to evaluate your results. This means ask yourself how much, if any, things have improved. Do you have more energy? Are you sleeping better? Or whatever your goals were.

If results can't be gotten by tuning in to your body, then dowse as needed to gauge the success. For example, if you did a round of digestive supplements to help you absorb your food better, you may not be sure if they are working, because you didn't have obvious symptoms. In cases like that, you can dowse your progress by testing the original question about your digestion and see if the results have improved. Hopefully you wrote the first answer down and dated it. That's why the charts at the end of each chapter have columns.

How GOOD Is Your Whole Supplement Program?

A mistake often made, even by professionals, is to only test a single supplement for effectiveness. But if you are taking any other supplements, it is important to test how adding that new supplement into your entire program is going to affect the overall performance of the program.

While the supplement may test as being very helpful for the particular symptom you have, its effectiveness may go down when combined with other supplements. Indeed, it could lower the effectiveness of other elements of your program. So after finding the best supplement, test the overall effectiveness of your entire supplement program when you add the new supplement to it. As long as it stays 8 or higher, you're fine.

What is the overall effectiveness of my entire program of supplements for my health goals at this time if I include this new product?

If the number has dropped below 8 on a scale of 10, you need to find another supplement to resolve the problem.

Why You Need To Dowse Your Supplements Regularly

Your body is constantly changing. Some days you need more help than others. As your health improves (we are assuming it will, since that is your goal), you will find that you can drop some items from your program. During times of increased stress, you will want to be open to adding some things temporarily. **Always check with your doctor before removing any prescription medication or changing dosages, as some require special programs for withdrawal.**

We suggest that about once a month, you test each individual supplement or remedy and drop any that are under 8 on a scale of 10. Put them aside, as you may need to add them back in later. Then, test the entire program and make sure it's still at least an 8. The idea is to create a program of supplements that have maximum impact on improving your health and immune strength while not taking any that are a waste of time or money.

It's true that anything you put into your body requires energy to be processed. So if you are taking supplements you don't need, you are making unnecessary work for your body. You don't want to do that.

Allergies

IDENTIFYING Allergies With Dowsing

You can be allergic or sensitive to substances that you ingest, breathe or contact. Often, if you are allergic to one item, you have allergies to others. Allergies and sensitivities feel very much alike in most cases, so we won't distinguish between them for the purpose of dowsing.

There are lists of common allergens online, and you can download one for evaluating yourself. You may have a suspicion or believe you are allergic to something, but put that from your mind and be detached while dowsing about it.

Scales are useful when evaluating allergies, because you will want to deal with allergens that have the most effect on you. We like to use a scale of 0-10 to show the intensity of allergic/sensitive response, with 0 being none and 10 being the most you could show.

For each item you want to test, ask:

How allergic/sensitive am I to _____ on a scale of 0 to 10, with 0 being not allergic at all and 10 being the most allergic I could be?

Make a note of which items you get 8 or higher for, if any. Those are the ones that you want to deal with first. Symptoms often begin to show at 3 or higher.

WHAT CAN You Do If You Have Allergies?

There are many paths you can take. Eliminating the allergen from your diet/environment is the first thing we would suggest.

Seek professional help for allergies that are serious or life-threatening, or if they prevent you from living a normal life.

Work on healing your liver, as often you will see an overloaded liver if there are a lot of allergies.

CHALLENGES IN ALLERGY Testing

It isn't always that straightforward to identify an allergen. For example, you may dowse as sensitive to melons, and you may react negatively when you eat them. But is it the melon itself, or is it the molds that are common in melons? Maggie was told by her doctor many years ago that it was just too difficult to track the causes of her allergies down, and he'd just write her a prescription for Seldane. This was unacceptable to her, so she went on to study and heal herself with the help of a variety of holistic practitioners and therapies, including dowsing.

If you find you are sensitive to a lot of fruits and veggies, maybe you are allergic to pesticide residues rather than the fruits and veggies themselves. Switching to organic will help you see which is the problem.

Not all ingredients are listed clearly in many processed foods. For example, garlic is a common allergen that is not always listed as an ingredient when present.

Other common examples of incomplete labeling include wheat gluten, which may be listed as 'vegetable starch', and paprika which may be listed as 'spice'.

We have found that people can actually be allergic to emotions and concepts. For example, you could be allergic to joy, success or financial wealth. If you find you have this type of an allergy, you can clear it the same way you do physical ones. The symptoms you get from allergies to concepts usually won't be physical.

. . .

Resolving The Energetic Causes Of Allergies

There are many fine methods for clearing allergies. Ones you can do yourself, if trained, include: EFT (Emotional Freedom Technique) and SRT (Spiritual Response Therapy). Or you could seek professional help of some kind.

If you are not trained in the above, and you don't want to seek professional help, we have found that dowsing about past lives that contributed to the allergic reaction and then clearing those lives is a good way to go, and it will often reduce or remove the allergic response. Since this guide is not about healing methods, we won't go into detail about that here. You can, however, see some details about dowsing past lives in a later section of this book.

Diet & Fitness

Evaluating Your Diet

The best diet is actually just a good eating style you can live with that will meet all your nutritional needs. Going on a diet to lose weight rarely works as a permanent solution for being fit and healthy. Instead, we suggest you find a way of eating that you can enjoy and stick with that gives you good health and fitness.

There is no one size fits all diet or lifestyle. For most people, a diet that is organic, non-GMO and has the fewest number of additives will be a good place to start.

Obviously, reducing or eliminating junk food, sugar, sodas and processed food is a good first step. Just doing that will cause you to lose weight and feel more energy. We have had excellent results with eliminating grains from our diet.

Do your due diligence about any particular eating plan or diet, then dowse its effectiveness for your goals.

Make a list of the goals you have for being on this diet, then dowse:

How effective on a scale of 0-10 would the _____*diet be for achieving my health and fitness goals at this time?*

An 8 or higher indicates something worth implementing. Or another way of asking it:

What would be the overall Level in Effects of my following the _____*diet on my health and fitness goals on a scale of +10 to -10?*

A negative number would mean that the diet would actually drive you backwards along the path toward your goals.

How Long To Diet?

Remember that you are constantly changing. Your body may love a particular diet now, but in a month, it may want a change. Check the value of your diet once a month. If it drops below an 8, perhaps you need to supplement something, or else find a new diet.

You can also dowse how long it will take to achieve your goals with this diet, for example, if you want to lose 10 pounds. Use a question like this:

How long will I need to be on the _____*diet to achieve my goal of losing ten pounds? More than one month? More than two? Etc.*

Is One Diet Better Than Others?

You are an individual, and your body knows what it needs. What works for one person may or may not work for you. Dowsing will help you evaluate what diet is worth implementing.

You are always better off with a well-rounded diet that includes all the basic things you need for proper nutrition. Don't follow the food pyramid put out by the government. That's a joke. People are discovering that grains are not a requirement, and in fact they are poor nutritionally and lead to a lot of symptoms. Good quality oils are essential. Organic and non-GMO foods are safest. Pastured, wild-caught and grass-fed meats are best nutritionally and ethically.

If your food is raised in a natural and humane manner, it will be more healthy for you. For example, stressed chickens don't make healthy eggs.

Vegetarian diets have been shown to lead to certain vitamin deficiencies, because a more natural human diet does include animal protein, and vegetables cannot mimic those exactly. If you choose a vegetarian diet, be sure to supplement to make up for that.

We feel that it is best not to regard dietary choice as a moral issue. That type of judgment seems to go along with certain dietary restrictions from ancient religions. As if eating meat on Friday is a sin, or mixing dairy with meat is morally wrong and leads to punishment. We are not making fun of religious dietary restrictions; we just caution you not to use them as a way of feeling superior. A vegetarian diet doesn't make you more spiritual than a meat-eater. If only it were that simple! Getting your foods from sustainable, humane and non-GMO sources shows what you care about. But try not to regard such choices as making you superior to those who do not agree with you.

EVALUATING Your Fitness Regime

You can use dowsing to evaluate the effectiveness of a particular fitness regime or type of exercise for you. Write down what your fitness goals are. Then dowse the various options you have, like Pilates, yoga, running, cardio, etc.

What is the overall level in effects for me of participating in
_____*as a means of reaching my fitness goals on a scale of +10 to -10, with 0 having no effect and positive numbers having increasingly positive effects?*

How long would I need to participate in _____*to reach my stated fitness goals? More than one month? More than two? Etc.*

WHICH TYPE Of Exercise Is Best For You?

There is no one-size-fits-all fitness regimen. Some people respond better to vigorous workouts, while others find that stressful and respond better to gentle programs like yoga. You can use dowsing to find out what will best suit you if you aren't sure.

Make a list of the types of exercise regimens you are considering. Then dowse each:

On a scale of +10 to -10, with 0 being neutral and positive numbers meaning I would enjoy success and negative numbers meaning I would dislike it/not get results, what is the value of participating in _____*for me at this time for my fitness goals and enjoyment?*

Choosing Therapies

FACTORS TO CONSIDER When Dowsing Therapies

You can dowse the effectiveness of a therapy for your goal. You can dowse one that you were inspired about, or you can dowse the one recommended by your health care professional. There are no one-size-fits-all therapies. That is why dowsing is so helpful. You can use dowsing to find out how effective it will be for you, your loved one or your pet.

Therapies sometimes have side effects, especially if they are allopathic in origin. You can use dowsing to determine the level of side effects, or just wrap that into the question when comparing possible therapies. It doesn't matter how good the therapy is for resolving your issue if it just creates other issues.

Sometimes it works out best to use more than one therapy. Sometimes you will see the best results if you do one therapy, then switch to another after a period of time. Dowsing will help you figure out which ones and when to use them.

WHICH THERAPY IS BEST?

Make a list of the therapies you want to consider. For example, when treating cancer, your doctor may tell you that you have an option of radiation, chemotherapy, medication, surgery, macrobiotic diet, and several other things.

Write down your goal. Be sure your goal is related to restoring balance and health, not just about getting rid of symptoms. Your goal is to be healthy, feel good and be able to function physically at a very high level. You want to pick the therapy that will get you closest to that goal.

You want to be detached about the results. Don't even bother dowsing if you are fearful or want to get a particular answer. You won't be accurate. In cases like that, you can blind dowse to avoid your emotional reaction if you don't have someone who can dowse for you who isn't attached to results. See the Appendix for how to blind dowse.

Considering all my goals and desiring a minimum of negative side effects, what is the overall level in effects of using _____(fill in the blank with a therapy) on a scale of +10 to -10 at this time as directed for my specific health goals (as listed), with a positive number meaning it will enhance health, 0 means neutral/no effect and a negative number meaning it will detract from health.

HOW LONG TO USE IT?

Every person is unique, so how long to use a therapy for best results will depend on the individual. While you probably won't be able to convince your doctor to do radiation or chemotherapy for the amount of time you dowse is best, you will find it useful to dowse how long to take a particular herb or homeopathic for best results.

Considering my specific health goals, what is the best length of time for me to use this therapy to restore balance and health and resolve the cause of my physical symptoms? More than one week? More than one month? Etc.

When you reach the length of time you have dowsed, you can retest to make sure it's still appropriate to quit the therapy. Then you can ask if there is another remedy or therapy that would be an 8 or higher on a scale of 10 for continuing the healing process.

EVALUATING **Results**

You don't always have to dowse to evaluate your results. In most cases, if you have picked an effective therapy or remedy, you will see a reduction in symptoms or a resolution of your problem. But sometimes you can't see or feel the change, so in that case, you can dowse efficacy before you start the therapy and then again after you have done it for the proper amount of time.

For example, if you dowsed that your digestive system had a level of inflammation that was a 7 out of 10, then you did a herbal anti-inflammatory and changed your diet for 30 days, you could retest the level of inflammation in your digestive system at the end of that time and see the change.

If the results still give you a number that shows there is an imbalance, you can work with your health care professional, or if you are a competent health dowser, you can dowse what to do next to continue the healing process.

When To Consult A Professional

DO YOU NEED PROFESSIONAL HELP?

One of the most useful applications for health dowsing is to help you decide when it is appropriate to invest time and money in professional health care services for you, a loved one or a beloved pet. Even if you have excellent health insurance, it is costly in terms of time to consult with a professional. And for veterinarian consultations and for those who lack insurance, knowing when to go to a doctor guarantees you don't waste money.

We routinely dowse to see if taking our pet to the vet is the most effective way to resolve a physical symptom. Our pets are quite healthy for the most part, and we can go a couple years without needing to see a vet even though we have 10 pets. In 2013, though, we had a few cases of accidents that caused us concern about 3 of our cats, and in each case, dowsing indicated going to the vet was unnecessary.

Knowing how much it costs to go to the vet, we certainly saved upwards of $1000 or more in vet bills that year through dowsing. And each of the 3 cats recovered very nicely without complications using simple methods available to us at home.

Although this is one of the most useful health dowsing applications, it is not wise to wait until you have a sick pet or child to dowse this question. Practice your dowsing all the time. Learn detachment. Check your answers. Gain confidence in your accuracy. Then when the time comes to dowse this subject, you will be able to get good answers.

Always have a good dowser back up your answers by dowsing for you. Get a second and third opinion and make sure you feel that the answers are accurate. **If in doubt, go to the doctor. Do not play games with the health of yourself or a loved one. Only good health dowsers should attempt to dowse this subject.**

• • •

Factors That Affect Your Decision

You probably never thought of it this way, but every time you or someone in your family is ill or has an accident, you make a conscious decision about whether to seek professional help. Sometimes that answer is obvious. You may have an allergy, or your child has the sniffles. You choose to use an over-the-counter remedy and your own knowledge of how to boost the immune system or reduce symptoms instead of going to the doctor, and everything goes well.

On another occasion, your child may fall from her bike, landing on her outstretched hand. The pain is obviously very bad, and the arm is swelling at an alarming rate. You rush her to the emergency room, because you are quite certain the arm or wrist is broken, and it is.

In both of those cases, you decided without dowsing whether it was appropriate to seek outside professional help. But what about the in-between cases? We've all had them happen from time to time.

My experience has been that people in such cases will follow their own judgment. Some will choose to err on the side of being overly cautious, because they wouldn't want to make a mistake and appear to be a bad parent. Others might take the opposite tack and refuse to seek help due to a sense of machismo, not wanting to appear weak, or maybe because they don't feel they should spend money on themselves. Whenever you make decisions based on reasons like these, it's easier for mistakes to happen.

Before you dowse about whether to seek outside help, make a list of factors that you would include in your decision. Not everyone has the same list, and that means that not everyone will get the same answer when they ask the question. Your answer will only be as accurate as the list you have made, so take the time to do it right.

Some factors you might include:

◆How much you feel you can afford to pay out of pocket (this might apply more in the case of a pet)

◆Whether you have the means at home to resolve this situation yourself

◆Whether you are as competent to deal with this situation yourself

◆Whether this is a potentially life-threatening situation

◆Whether your taking care of this situation will take longer than if you went to a doctor

◆Whether going to a doctor would speed the recovery process and go easier on the patient

Once you have a complete list, you can dowse your question:

Considering the factors that matter the most to me, what is the overall level in effects of consulting a health care professional about this situation on a scale of +10 to -10, with positive numbers meaning good outcomes and 0 meaning no effect and negative meaning a bad result.

Then ask the question this way and compare the answers:

Considering the factors that matter most to me, what is the overall level in effects of NOT consulting a health care professional about this situation, but instead using methods known to or accessible by me, on a scale of +10 to -10, with positive numbers indicating a good outcome and 0 being no effect and negative numbers meaning a bad outcome.

Usually you will end up with 2 very different numbers. If one is positive and the other 0 or negative, go with the positive choice. If one is much more positive than the other, choose that. If they are very close, we would suggest looking at your list and seeing if you can think of any other factors that matter to you, add them in and re-dowse the questions.

If it appears no matter how you define it that either choice is ok, you can verify that by dowsing:

Does it make any difference in terms of outcome whether I consult a professional or deal with this situation myself?

If there is no real difference between each option, just go with whatever feels best to you.

WHICH PROFESSIONAL TO Choose

If you don't have a regular doctor, or if you want to compare health care providers, because you aren't certain whom to consult, then dowsing can help you a lot.

Make a list of your reasons and goals for consulting a professional. Then make a list of the potential doctors and dowse this question:

Considering my specific health goals and desiring the best, quickest, most lasting positive outcome with minimal side effects, what is the overall level in effects on a scale of +10 to -10 of consulting Dr. _____about this situation?

Get a number for each potential doctor by dowsing every name on your list. We recommend 8 or higher as the cutoff for taking action.

If none of the candidates is 8 or higher, then add to the list of doctors or go back and look at your specific health goals and see if maybe you should alter them. For example, if you have listed a goal of 'curing' a condition, then perhaps it cannot be cured as such. Maybe it can only be alleviated, and if so, none of the doctors would test 8 or higher, because a cure isn't possible.

EVALUATING Results

As with all dowsing, you want to evaluate your results. It is the chief way of improving your dowsing. As with many health issues, you won't always have to dowse to evaluate your results. You may find yourself smiling at the doctor's amazing bedside manner and insights, and that will help you confirm you dowsed well.

On the other hand, if you are not happy with how things are going, if you don't feel you are getting the results you expected, then it is wise to go back and look at your list of goals and see if you feel the question was a good one. Or you may have been too attached to results, and your dowsing wasn't accurate for that reason.

Child & Pet Health

FACTORS THAT ARE Different With Children And Animals

Small children and pets cannot tell you what's wrong or what hurts. Dowsing is a very useful tool to have in your kit when working with small children or animals.

Often, handling a pet who feels bad only adds to the stress the animal is feeling. If you can use dowsing to get an overall picture of what's going on, that will limit the amount of time you have to spend handling the animal.

Often, when children are ill or coming down with something, they will have bad behavior that shows you something is out of balance. The same is true of animals, who often will exhibit negative behavior when they are in pain. An example is a cat peeing outside of the litter box when he has a bladder infection. Remember that bad behavior is usually a cry for help, so take the time to find out what's going on.

PERMISSION IS STILL NEEDED

When dowsing for a child or pet in your care, you are within our definition of ethical behavior. However, you still need to make sure you have their permission to dowse about them, or your work may be a waste of time.

For a child, ask if she minds you trying to help her feel better. You'll hardly ever get a 'no' answer. Explain only in as much detail as necessary to let the child know your intentions. Don't overwhelm or scare her into thinking she might get a shot, have to take pills or go to a doctor. If you sense reluctance, you may need to let the child talk about what's causing that feeling. Maybe a past experience being sick or going to a doctor left a bad impression.

For a pet, you can dowse if you have the animal's permission to help him get well. If you get a 'yes', which you will get most of the time, proceed. Of course, you can't talk it over with a pet if the pet says 'no'. It is rare that you won't get permission to help your pet.

What do you do if you can't get permission? Well, if you feel it is necessary to get help or do something to help your patient, do it. But be aware that a reluctant patient will usually not heal as quickly. It is important to acknowledge free will. There is no harm in continuing to offer assistance, and you have to follow your own judgment in health care situations. Don't ignore an obvious health issue just because the patient doesn't want treatment.

Being Detached Can Be Difficult…But It's Necessary

One of the most important reasons to dowse all the time is that it helps you develop a sense of detachment, and that is vital when dowsing about health issues. You can't expect to dowse well about important health issues if you don't dowse often. So practice your dowsing as much as possible, and cultivate a sense of curiosity about answers. It takes time, but it will increase your accuracy.

Teach Your Children To Dowse

Children take to dowsing particularly well. In fact, children are excellent at natural healing and energy techniques. We had a client who had a 3-yr-old who quickly learned to ask for EFT (Emotional Freedom Technique) when she was feeling out of balance.

If you teach your children to dowse, they will be able to participate in their healing process. It is terrific to get children empowered to use their intuitive sensing abilities and feel their health is something they can affect.

Make dowsing a game and fun for your children. Finding hidden objects is a good game. Having them dowse what color to wear for a certain outcome is fun. Slowly get them dowsing about things they have an opinion about, and teach them detachment, so they learn to listen to their intuition.

EUTHANASIA OF PETS

One of the most heart-wrenching situations for pet owners is when an older pet seems to have reached the end of her life. Often, the vet will say it's time to put the animal down. But some part of you isn't sure.

While it is often true that euthanasia is the appropriate choice, we have seen many situations where it was not. And by being able to use dowsing and follow their inner guidance, the pet owner had many more months, sometimes years, of quality time with their animal companion.

One example was my mother's German Shepherd, Sam. The vet told her the dog was old and had an inflammation of the spine which made it very hard for her to stand and walk, and it was not going to get better. He said to put the dog to sleep. My Mom came to me, and I did some dowsing and had her put the dog on a curcumin extract pill. The dog recovered the use of her hind end and lived happily for another 18 months, at which time she died of other causes.

We have had many pets in our lives, and on occasion, we have had to make a decision about euthanasia. We use dowsing to help us understand a number of factors that contribute to the decision. You can just dowse if it's appropriate based on your values and goals. Or you can go into more detail and find out what's going on with your beloved pet. Sometimes, more information is useful for making your decision.

We may sound like a broken record when we say you need to write all your goals down before dowsing, but once again, everyone has their own values about this subject. It isn't universal truth. Some people may have to consider whether the animal is incontinent, and they have no way of caring for an incontinent pet. Others may not feel they can leave a seriously ill or disabled animal alone all day while they go to work. Or some may have physical challenges that make it impossible to carry a large pet outside several times a day to go to the bathroom. Or they simply feel they don't have the resources to care for a seriously handicapped or ill elderly animal.

Some people don't care how much it costs; they will keep their pet with them as long as the pet is happy and wants to stay. Others may feel they have to consider the cost of pills and special feeding and such.

Make your list of what matters to you in this decision. It may include factors such as:

◆How much time you have to care for a sick pet

◆How strong you are

◆How much money you have

◆How much help you have for this project

◆Whether the pet wants to stay here

◆How much pain the pet is in

◆If the pet can get well enough to enjoy life for a time

◆Is the vet correct that the pet cannot improve and has no quality of life

Once you are very clear about the factors that matter for you, then you know what should contribute to a 'yes' answer and what would swing it to 'no' when you ask about euthanizing your pet.

Considering all the factors that matter to me, is it appropriate at this time to euthanize _____(name of pet)?

If you don't want to jump right to dowsing about that question, the following are dowsing questions you can ask that might give you information that could lead to other avenues you might want to pursue at this time:

◆*On a scale of 0-10, with 0 being no pain and 10 being the most she can feel, what level of pain is my pet experiencing on average at this time?*

◆*Does my pet feel she can recover and be healthy and feel good? (Sometimes pets are sick so long, they can't picture getting well, and that blocks them from healing).*

◆*Does my pet want to move on/leave the planet at this time?*

◆*Does my pet want to stay here with me? Is it only because she knows how bad I will feel without her? (Often they will choose to stay out of a sense of duty even when they are suffering).*

◆*Is there any treatment, therapy or program that I can find and financially afford that would heal my pet and restore her to feeling comfortable?*

Depending on the answers you get, you might decide to pursue a second opinion on your pet's condition, or to do more research about options, the way my Mom did. However, you often discover that the pet is only hanging around because she knows how torn up you are about losing her. Pets are often more willing to move on than we are to let them go.

This is not always the case, however. Our dog India did not want to leave us, even when she had no quality of life. She was incontinent; couldn't eat or drink without vomiting; was in pain; couldn't walk. And still, she did not want to leave us.

We worked on ourselves, thinking it was us keeping her here, but it turned out she just didn't want to go. We told her she could come back to us as another pet in the future if she wanted to. It was hard to euthanize her, knowing she did not want to go, but it was very helpful being able to dowse in detail, and we felt we did the right thing at the right time. And in the end, that is really what you need and want most. You just want to do the best you can by your beloved pet.

Evaluating The Cause Of A Symptom

LONG TERM LEVEL In Effects Of What's Going On

One of the biggest gifts we can share with you about health in general is to help you see symptoms in a new way. Just because something is painful does not mean it is bad. It just means things are a bit chaotic or out of balance.

Even though you know this is true, you do not tend to apply that knowledge in health situations. If you hurt, you think something is wrong. Yet, if you just began a fitness program, don't your muscles usually cry out in pain the next day? Does that mean you need a doctor? No, of course not. You know better.

So why when you get an unexplained pain do you imagine some terrible health problem? Probably because pain is generally regarded as negative. But pain is just a symptom of an imbalance. It may be a sign of disease, or it might actually be something that leads to a positive outcome, like sore muscles after a workout.

You can dowse about any symptom you have, whether it is pain or discomfort or a rash. Here's the question we use:

On a scale of +10 to -10, where a positive number means an overall positive outcome, what is the long term level in effects on my health and well-being of the process that includes _____(the current symptom)?

WHEN THE ANSWER IS NEGATIVE...

A negative number means that the symptom is part of a process that has an overall negative impact on your long term health. The bigger the number, the more serious it is.

A negative number might indicate a disease process, like a virus or bacterial infection. It might represent food poisoning or other toxicity. It could indicate a parasitic overgrowth/infection.

If you get a negative number, then you will want to treat the cause of the problem so you can resolve the symptoms and the process. You can dowse to see what therapy or remedy will best resolve the cause.

When It's Positive...

If on the other hand, the answer is a positive number, then, like sore muscles after a workout, your symptoms are a sign of a process that has a long term positive overall effect on your health. The bigger the number, the more positive it is.

Positive processes can be things like a detox, a healing crisis or a transformative process of some type.

If you get a positive number, you want to support the process and make it as comfortable as possible without stopping it. You can dowse to see what therapy or remedy will best support the process and allow it to bring positive results to you, while minimizing discomfort.

Finding The Cause

In most cases, if you can dowse the best way to resolve or support the process, it really doesn't matter that much what the original cause is. However, sometimes it can be useful or even important to know the cause. Chart or list dowsing is a good way to determine causes. Always be sure 'other' is an option, as no list is complete.

A cause could be physical, like an infection or trauma. Or it could be energetic, like a chakra link or aura damage. There are so many possible causes, it is beyond the scope of this book to list them all. You can make a list of those you are familiar with and dowse it.

Once you discover the cause, you can dowse what the best therapy or remedy to resolve it will be. Remember to only apply things that rank 8 or higher on a scale of 10, for best results.

~

All The Health Questions

On a scale of +10 to -10, with 0 being average for my gender, age and culture, what is my overall physical health at this time?

On a scale of +10 to -10, with 0 being average for my gender, age and culture, what is the overall physical health of my _____ System at this time?

On a scale of +10 to -10, with 0 being average for my gender, age and culture, what is the overall physical health of my _____ at this time?

On a scale of 0 to 10, with 0 being none and 10 being the worst/most it could be, what is the level/degree of physical_____ in my physical body at this time?

Are there any _____at this time in my aura that are having a significant effect on the health and well-being of my aura?

On a scale of 0 to 100%, with 100% being the best and most optimal functioning, what is the value of my EM Field as an average over the last 7 days?

Is red/blue/purple/silver/gold the best color for me to use to repair, restore and strengthen my EM Field at this time?

Will supplementation by any of these products be an 8 or higher on a scale of 10 (with 10 being the most helpful) for creating excellent immune balance, good energy levels and excellent physical function for my body at this time when taken as directed?

Are any of these products an 8 or higher on a scale of 10 for reaching my overall health goals at this time when taken as directed?

How long would it be best for me to take this supplement to reach my health goals: More than 30 days? More than 60 days? More than 90 days?

How many bottles of this supplement taken at the suggested dosage will be required for me to reach my health goals? 1? 2? 3?

What is the overall effectiveness of my entire program of supplements for my health goals at this time if I include this new product?

How allergic/sensitive am I to _____ on a scale of 0 to 10, with 0 being not allergic at all and 10 being the most allergic I could be?

How effective on a scale of 0-10 would the _____diet be for achieving my health and fitness goals at this time?

What would be the overall Level in Effects of my following the _____diet on my health and fitness goals on a scale of +10 to -10?

How long will I need to be on the _____diet to achieve my goal of losing ten pounds? More than one month? More than two? Etc.

What is the overall level in effects for me of participating in _____as a means of reaching my fitness goals on a scale of +10 to -10, with 0 having no effect and positive numbers having increasingly positive effects?

How long would I need to participate in _____to reach my stated fitness goals? More than one month? More than two? Etc.

On a scale of +10 to -10, with 0 being neutral and positive numbers meaning I would enjoy success and negative numbers meaning I would dislike it/not get results, what is the value of participating in _____for me at this time for my fitness goals and enjoyment?

Considering all my goals and desiring a minimum of negative side effects, what is the overall level in effects of using _____(fill in the blank with a therapy) on a scale of +10 to -10 at this time as directed for my specific health goals (as listed), with a positive number meaning it will enhance health and a negative number meaning it will detract from health.

Considering my specific health goals, what is the best length of time for me to use this therapy to restore balance and health and resolve the cause of my physical symptoms? More than one week? More than one month? Etc.

Considering the factors that matter the most to me, what is the overall level in effects of consulting a health care professional about this situation on a scale of +10 to -10, with positive numbers meaning good outcomes and 0 meaning no effect.

Considering the factors that matter most to me, what is the overall level in effects of NOT consulting a health care professional about this situation, but instead using methods known to or accessible by me, on a scale of +10 to -10, with positive numbers indicating a good outcome and 0 being no effect and negative numbers meaning a bad outcome.

Considering my specific health goals and desiring the best, quickest, most lasting positive outcome with minimal side effects, what is the overall level in effects on a scale of +10 to -10 of consulting Dr. _____about this situation?

Considering all the factors that matter to me, is it appropriate at this time to euthanize _____(name of pet)?

- On a scale of 0-10, with 0 being no pain and 10 being the most she can feel, what level of pain is my pet experiencing on average at this time?

- Does my pet feel she can recover and be healthy and feel good? (Sometimes pets are sick so long, they can't picture getting well, and that blocks them from healing).

- Does my pet want to move on/leave the planet at this time?

- Does my pet want to stay here with me? Is it only because she knows how bad I will feel without her? (Often they will choose to stay out of a sense of duty).

- Is there any treatment, therapy or program that I can find and afford to apply financially that would heal my pet and restore her to feeling comfortable?

On a scale of +10 to -10, where a positive number means an overall positive outcome, what is the long term level in effects on my health and well-being of the process that includes _____(the current symptom)?

$\sim$

Dowsing Deeper

THE QUESTIONS in this book have helped us transform our lives; save lots of money; become healthier and more successful. But can you improve on them? Of course you can!

Each person is an individual. You have your own point of view made up of your values, beliefs and how you define and rate things in terms of your preferences.

Your dowsing question will be affected by all these things. A question asked using Maggie Percy's definitions of terms and her goals will be a good question for her, but it may or may not be a perfect question for you.

The best way to be sure to get dowsing answers that work for you is to create your own questions. This section will guide you in how to do that. It's only for serious dowsers who really want to improve their accuracy, because they intend to use dowsing to make their life better, or to help others.

We believe that learning to ask good dowsing questions not only improves your dowsing; it makes you think about your beliefs, values and preferences, and that causes you to live more consciously, to question things and to actively choose to create the life you want.

WHAT ARE YOUR GOALS?

Not everyone has the exact same goals. Some people don't even really HAVE goals. So the first thing to do is to know your goals and to think about them in detail, so that when you create a dowsing question, you have a clear purpose for asking it, and you are aiming to achieve your goals.

Good goals are detailed and personal. You can ask what is healthy for you, or what will make you healthier, but what do you mean by that? Do you want to eliminate pain? Do you want to be able to have lots of energy? Do you want to run a marathon easily?

Think about the subject you are dowsing about, and ask yourself exactly what you hope to achieve by using a therapy, taking a supplement or consulting a doctor. What is the positive outcome you wish to create?

List the things that you consider important factors in your dowsing answer. For example, some people feel they can't spend more than a certain amount of money. If that is true for you, put it clearly in your list. You may really care about consulting a professional who will want your participation, rather than pushing you around. If so, put that on the list.

.   .   .

What Do Your Words Mean?

Too often, you use words that you haven't clearly defined. You may think you know what they mean, but you don't. If you use vague, undefined terms, your answer won't necessarily be accurate for you.

We spoke earlier of not using vague terms like "good", "healthy", "highest and greatest good". These words and phrase have vague meanings, or none at all. Don't use them.

Instead, think about words that mean something specific to you and relate to your goals. "Having enough energy to do whatever I feel like", "feeling physically good and comfortable", "improving my memory significantly" are examples of specific terms and phrases.

People use poor words when they are lazy, or if they lack confidence or just are living unconsciously. Dowsing will help you question your values and get you to act more consciously, which will help you manifest positive outcomes.

Don't use other people's definitions of terms unless you are sure you agree with them.

Include All The Parts Of A Good Question

Poor questions often are poor because they lack an important element. A good question should include how, what, where, when, who and why.

Time is a critical aspect that is often overlooked. "At this time" is a good phrase to add to any question when you are testing something for right now.

Indicate whom you are dowsing the therapy/supplement/remedy for.

Include when you intend to apply what you are dowsing about, and for how long.

Add in as appropriate how often or what dosage you will be using.

Be sure to include why you are asking the question; what is the goal.

A good dowsing question is usually long and detailed.

CHECK **Your Answers**

As often as possible, write down your question and your answer, and then after an appropriate time, check your answer for accuracy.

Sometimes the answer is accurate, but you left out an important part, so it appears to be wrong. Here's an example: Maggie dowsed that she would be given approval for a home loan modification. She had gone through a laborious process with Bank of America, and it dowsed that a home loan modification would be approved.

But she left something out. She left out 'when'. Because she was caught up in the filing of paperwork and was very focused on the present process, it didn't occur to her to add a time.

BAC rejected the application after 18 months of haggling. Maggie couldn't believe her dowsing, which had felt so accurate, was wrong, but she had to accept facts.

Then, 3 years later, the mortgage was sold to another company, who approached Maggie about applying for a home loan modification. Not being keen on going through 18 months of trouble, she was hesitant, but did it anyway. Within 3 months, approval came through, and the modification was granted.

Maggie's dowsing was right, but she only found that out later. Look at your question. If it appears wrong, ask yourself if you included ALL the aspects of a good question. Ask yourself how you could change the question and have it be correct. If Maggie had done that exercise, she might have realized that maybe the answer WAS correct, but not for that case.

Making mistakes is a great way to improve your dowsing if you take the time to check your answers and find ways to improve how you ask questions. Don't be upset if you make a mistake...learn from it!

STUDY **Your Subject**

If you want to be a good health dowser, study about the physical body, how it works and learn about organs, systems and ailments. Read about allergies and different diets. Get some good books with illustrations of anatomy. An anatomy coloring book can be quite useful. Find a health guru who resonates with you and subscribe to her blog. Read books related to physical health. The more you know, the better your questions will be. You don't have to have 2 Biology degrees like Maggie, but it can be a real blessing.

5

CAREER & LIFE PATH QUESTIONS

Overview

WHY ARE YOU HERE?

Whether you realize it or not, one of the biggest questions in your life, one that runs through your life like a thread is "Why Am I Here?". We all hunger for a meaning, a purpose. Often, it takes decades before that hunger really kicks in. If you started early on this subject, you're one of the lucky ones. And dowsing can help guide you.

Each person has their own unique purpose in life. It isn't always as easy as finding something you are talented at and doing it. You are lucky if you are good at music, sports, public speaking or numbers. Having a traditional gift and pursuing it is satisfying and rewarding. But not everyone finds that they have a conventional gift that they can study in school or learn to do better.

All of us came here to experience various things, but no two people have the same agenda. You might have come here specifically to learn to step into your power; to set good boundaries; to give and receive in equal measure; or all of them. Maybe you are here to settle several karmic debts or resolve unfinished karmic business. Perhaps you came here to learn the value of letting go of emotional baggage.

Most people have many agendas, and those goals weave together in an intricate web. We attract the people who will help us reach our goals, and often one person may play many roles in that. Some have come to help you, while others have come to oppose you so that you can learn the value of standing up for what you believe.

Almost everyone is here to learn that separation is an illusion and to learn to love him- or herself. Just experiencing love of all kinds is a gift and a blessing of being here.

How Dowsing Can Help

Since dowsing expands our ability to get accurate answers and useful guidance, this is a particular area where dowsing shines. It will challenge you to accept and follow through on your answers, because often, it will take a long time to see the results.

Practice dowsing and become confident so that you can do what your dowsing says without reservation. It will lead to better results overall than just using your left brain to make decisions.

Outside Help vs. Dowsing

It's fun to consult psychics and other intuitives about what you are meant to do. Sometimes they can be uncannily accurate. But the bottom line is that, although we all need outside help at times, and it's good to consult experts of all kinds, it is also important to learn to trust your heart about the major life choices you have.

So by all means go to your favorite tarot card reader for advice. But also dowse. Ask your Inner Guru what's best for you. No one, absolutely no one, knows what's best for you better than you do. And dowsing is one of the best ways to get in touch with your Inner Guru.

Evaluating Blocks To Success

WHAT ARE Your Blocks To Success?

There are many possible blocks to success in your career and life path. Dowsing will help you identify them and also see how much of an impact they are having on your goals.

It is common for people to doubt their own abilities, to lack confidence and to fear jealousy of other less successful people. These are just a few dowsing questions aimed at seeing what some of the key blocks are that you may have.

On all levels of my being, do I believe...

I am good enough to succeed?

It's safe for me to succeed?

The Universe will support me and help me succeed?

My family and loved ones want me to succeed?

I have all the talents I need to succeed?

On any level of my being, do I believe...

Others will reject me if I succeed?

My family will reject me if I succeed?

Others will be jealous of me if I succeed?

I will be killed if I succeed?

Success will ruin my life?

I will not go to heaven if I succeed?

I am only spiritual because I am poor?

. . .

How Big Is The Impact? Dowsing Intensity Of Blocks

As with any dowsing question, you can use scales to see how strong a particular block is. Obviously, bigger numbers mean bigger blocks. We use a scale of 0-10 to measure intensity, with anything over an 8 being serious.

If you dowsed a question from the list above, like "On some level of my being, I believe I will be killed if I succeed." And you dowse:

On a scale of 0-10, how big an impact is this belief having on my ability to succeed at my goals?

You can ignore those with very low numbers, like below 3. But anything that is 8 or higher will have a strong effect.

Do You Sabotage Yourself?

Subconscious issues and beliefs that create and support low self-esteem and self-loathing will lead you to make poor choices and sabotage yourself. You will wonder why you can't make progress, but the self-sabotage is just an effort by your subconscious to keep you safe.

Once you identify these issues, you can clear them using whatever clearing method you like best. You can dowse which of the methods you know will be most effective.

You can check where you are with respect to positive beliefs about yourself by dowsing:

On a scale of 0-10, with 10 being best, how much do I believe on all levels that I have all the talent it takes to succeed at my goals?

On a scale of 0-10, with 10 being best, how much do I agree (on all levels of my being) that I am intelligent enough to achieve my goals?

On a scale of 0-10, with 10 being best, how much am I in alignment on all levels of my being with my goals about my career?

On a scale of 0-10, with 10 being best, how much confidence do I have overall in my ability to achieve my goals?

On a scale of 0-10, with 0 being best, how much energy am I holding at any level that is not in alignment with my current career goals?

ARE PAST LIVES AFFECTING YOU?

Whether you know it or not, whether you believe it or not, other lifetimes are having an effect on this one. However, that is not an ideal situation. Subconscious beliefs, energetic connections, old vows and cellular memory carry the energies of other lives. Those energies often cause you trouble in this life.

The worst past life situations are those that ended in death or serious trauma to you or a loved one. In those lives, you created strong beliefs due to powerful emotions. And those beliefs almost always are false. Often created at the time of death, these beliefs are carried into this life and hinder your ability to live freely.

Here's an example: In a past life, you were a rich person. You lived in a society where there were a lot of poor people, and they were treated badly. Maybe you even treated them badly. A time of chaos came, and the poor rose up and killed the rich, and you were one of the casualties. At the time you died, you thought, "If only I hadn't been rich, I wouldn't have died." That belief changes over the years to: "If I am rich, I will be killed."

Experiences from other lives rarely have any truth in this life, but unless you find and clear them, they can block you. Your negative beliefs about success that are tied to past lives where your success at gaining wealth, power and status led to your death will block you from succeeding in this lifetime.

You can learn more about clearing beliefs in the next chapter.

Sometimes, when you are trying to accomplish a goal in this life, your subconscious checks its data bank and finds a similar life to decide what might happen. And sometimes, you end up connecting to that other life energetically. You might consciously think if only you could connect to another life where you were good at _____, this life would be better, because your success would be faster. This is a mistake. You cannot only connect to the 'good stuff' from other lives.

See the section on Past Lives in the next chapter for more details on this subject.

A good general starting question is:

Am I currently being negatively affected in my career goals by other lifetimes?

How much on a scale of 10, with 0 being no effect, am I being impacted negatively by other lives at this time in my career goals?

Check out the section in the next chapter if you get significant results to the above questions.

Do You Have Trouble Knowing What You Want?

Not knowing what your gift is can be a reflection of your trying to please others instead of yourself. If you know your gift, you may be concerned at some level that your family won't support you. Or maybe you know what your passion is, but you can't make yourself pursue it. The same reasons may apply.

You can usually answer these questions without dowsing. If the answers show a pattern of people-pleasing and fear of rejection or judgment, you would benefit from working to release those attitudes. That will allow your gift to show itself. And you will have more confidence about living your passion.

True or False:

On any level of my being, do I believe I must do what my parents want me to do?

On any level of my being, do I believe that I cannot have what I want?

On any level of my being, do I believe it is selfish for me to do what I want?

On any level of my being, do I doubt that I have enough talent to successfully express my gift?

On any level of my being, do I believe I cannot support myself with my gift?

On any level of my being, do I believe I will be rejected if I live my passion?

On any level of my being, do I fear the judgment of my family for living my passion?

On any level of my being, do I believe that I will attract jealousy from those close to me if I express my gift?

On any level of my being, do I fear the results of expressing my gift?

On any level of my being, do I feel I have to let others dictate what I do?

∽

What Is Your Gift?

IF YOU KNOW What Your Gift Is...

The previous section had a short introduction to problems relating to your gift. If you believe you know what your gift is, and you are living your passion, you don't need this section.

If you believe you know what you want to do with your life, but you aren't doing it, then this section is for you. There may be various types of blocks causing you to hesitate to share your gift and live your passion. Often, they relate to fear of rejection and seeing yourself through others' eyes instead of having a vision of yourself.

You can test these statements and see which relate to your blocks:

At the subconscious level, do I believe that expressing my gift will cause others to reject me?

At the subconscious level, do I believe my gift is valuable?

At the subconscious level, do I believe that following my passion and expressing my gift can support me financially?

At the subconscious level, am I afraid of what others will think if I express my gift and live my passion?

At the subconscious level, do I have any blocks to expressing my gift and living my passion?

At the subconscious level, do I have fear about the effects of expressing my gift and living my passion?

On all levels, do I feel competent to support myself by living my passion?

Are you aware of any family patterns where you have been told you can't make a living doing what you love? When Maggie was in 7th grade, she expressed a strong desire to write. Both of her parents told her she couldn't make a living doing that, and she would need to find other work. She dropped her dreams of writing and only came back to them decades later.

Have you been affected by family or societal beliefs?

Do I believe on any level of my being that I cannot make a living doing what I love?

Do I believe on any level of my being that my gift is not valuable enough to sell it?

Am I expressing at any level family beliefs or patterns that say you can't succeed by doing what you love?

You will have some conscious awareness of how your family affected your beliefs. But you won't know how strongly the subconscious is affecting you until you dowse about it. Often, a slight agreement on the conscious level mirrors a very strong subconscious belief. Dowsing allows you to see the source of the beliefs that are creating your reality.

You may not think your family had that much of an effect on you. But they did. And it's ok. Because you can live the life you want to rather than be limited by what your family believed.

If You Don't Know **What Your Gift Is...**

Everyone has a gift. But we are brought up to think a gift is like a musical or athletic talent. If you can't play an instrument or a game, what is your talent? Are you drawn to writing? Do you love public speaking? No?

You are one of the lucky ones if you have a talent that is recognized by society. Art, music, sports, acting, writing, healing: these are all things of value. Maggie spent so many years feeling lost, because she didn't have a classically recognized talent, and she was eager to know what her gift was. For many years, she felt she had no gift.

But what she found was that there are many more gifts than society talks about. Maybe your gift is that you are a good listener. Or maybe you are able to hear the truth. Perhaps you have the gift of being able to calm any situation. Or you are an incredible mediator.

The gifts most of us have are NOT of the common variety, so we think we have none.

Everyone has a gift. It won't always make you rich. It won't always make you famous. But it will always give you satisfaction, success and happiness if you find and use it.

Your gift may be so narrow in focus that you don't recognize it. But whatever your gift is, it has the power to create success in your life if you share it with others.

Some of the blocks to knowing what your gift is relate to not recognizing your talent. People often don't feel they are talented, and so they won't see their talent. They won't hear anyone praising them. Whether your talent is something obvious like a musical one or unusual and narrow, you won't see it if you don't want to. So you can use dowsing to discover your blocks to accepting your talent and recognizing it.

On all levels, do I accept that I am gifted?

On all levels, am I willing to accept that my talent exists and can help lots of people?

On all levels, am I willing to acknowledge my gifts?

Am I afraid to accept that I am gifted?

Do I fear negative consequences if I know what my gifts are?

Am I afraid that I will have to do something I don't want to if I acknowledge my gifts?

Do I feel safer ignoring my gifts than accepting and using them?

~

Job Offers

WHAT JOB TO GO AFTER?

You're going to get tired of hearing this, but the first thing you need to do is list your goals for seeking a job. If all you are thinking about is survival, then you will find a job, and you will survive, but you won't be happy and you won't achieve your other goals.

Write down all your goals. What are your long term plans? Do you want a job that will be interesting and stimulating? Do you want to be in management? What income are you aiming for? What lifestyle are you trying to create? How much free time do you want? Be specific.

Once you are clear about your goals, you can test the value of different job offers, and save yourself a lot of trouble in applications.

On a scale of +10 to -10, with positive numbers being good results, what is

evel in effects for my goals of applying for
_____*(name the job)?*

We would only apply for jobs that rank +8 or higher. Less than that
will give challenges. You can dowse each attribute on your goal list to
find out where each job is weakest or strongest.

SHOULD YOU ACCEPT THAT OFFER?

Now you have been offered a job. You have looked at the list of things
included in the offer. Your left brain can make an evaluation of the
value of this job.

But you are not done if you don't consult your heart. Dowsing allows
you to see how likely you are to feel good about this choice in the
future. Make your rational evaluation. Dismiss an offer if you see it
ranks very low. But if it ranks well, or if you feel intuitively that it
might be good, then the next step is to dowse about it.

*On a scale of +10 to -10, with positive numbers being good results, how happy
would I be in* _____*(name a time, like 5 years) if I accept the job and the
current terms offered, considering my goals?*

The use of asking future happiness is a good trick for any major
decision. You are often surprised at the results. Don't accept anything
that tests less than +8.

IS IT TIME TO Move On?

You're in a job you hate, or you really don't like. What do you do? You
have all kinds of excuses why changing jobs now isn't a good idea.
Don't listen to them. If you are not living your dream; if you aren't
happy with your job, you need to move on.

It will be more challenging if you are older or are in a tiny niche. But
focus on what you want to be creating instead of what you are

creating. What would you like to be experiencing? Do you want to have more freedom? Do you want to have greater appreciation? Make a list of the things that matter to you. If your current job isn't satisfying you, it's time to move on.

You can use dowsing as noted above to find new opportunities and evaluate them. Don't allow yourself to be stuck in a dead end job.

WHAT ABOUT CHANGES Of Career Late In Life?

When we reach a certain age, we are afraid to move on. I have heard SO many people say, "I'm only 5 years from retirement, and I get a good package." They are willing to bargain 5 or more years of life for a package that may or may not be there when they retire.

They are willing to hope they are still alive in 5 years and able to enjoy and live life. All anyone has is today. If you are not happy with your job or career NOW, it's time to make a change. If you are only 2 weeks from retirement and all that offers, fine. But do you really want to waste years of your life after wasting years already? So often, people wake up and realize they have wasted many years, but they stay in the job because they are close to retirement.

We believe in being rational; but we also believe in acting in integrity. If you are almost to retirement, like 1 month away, it's ok to hang in there if you want. But don't rationalize staying for years. That ridiculous. We don't know how much time we have. Live for the NOW.

~

Your Life's Purpose

YEARS ago we took a workshop with Anneliese Hagemann about our Life's Purpose. She offers a great affordable workbook on the subject that we highly recommend. You may visit this page to order it:

http://jvz7.com/c/37400/34031

We suggest you use Anneliese's material for this subject, as it is very thorough and we see no reason to duplicate it. There is a link in the Resources section to this book and her health dowsing book.

Your Life Has Many Purposes

Perhaps more than any other subject covered in this book, your life's purpose won't let you avoid it. Maybe you've always known what it was, drawn to it even as a child. Or maybe you've been seeking it for years, because it isn't something obvious in the values of your culture.

When you meet it, your life's purpose will grab you and never let you go. You'll think it was the opposite, that you found it and passionately embraced it. Either way, the passion you feel is not like infatuation with another human. It doesn't lead you wrong. You can trust that feeling of wanting to throw yourself into it, because you intuitively know you are right.

Your heart and your intuition want you to find your purpose in life. Dowsing is a great asset in helping you refine your choices, but in this subject, your intuition is usually so strong, you don't need a lot of dowsing.

Your Path May Change Over Time

It's not like your life has only one purpose. At any given time, there may be one focus. But your life may have many, many purposes.

In other words, your life has a particular purpose right now, and you can dowse to find out more about it. But don't feel that it is a one-time job. Maybe you are one of the lucky ones, and you found your calling early, and you love it and have lived it fully your whole life.

Not everyone has that experience. Don't judge yourself if you aren't sure what your purpose is, if you try lots of different roles to see what fits best. When you find the right thing, you will know. In fact, if you aren't sure, you probably haven't found it. You don't usually need to dowse to confirm your choice.

While some people are lucky that they follow a straight path to their life's purpose, others do not. Especially if you have a calling that is not part of the conventionally accepted array of careers in your culture, you may wander aimlessly from job to job, wondering why you can't find anything that you are passionate about.

This was what happened to Maggie. She had lots of different jobs, but none held her. Some she loved; some she hated. But she never felt any was her special calling.

Then she had a health collapse which totally changed the path she was on. After seven years of studying and learning new things, she finally moved across country and fell into a whole new reality. From the world of science and logic, she ended up in the world of energy healing and metaphysics. And she knew she had found her place.

But it was a series of experiences, a sort of spiritual evolution, that took place. She fell in love with Reiki and studied and practiced it, then was introduced to dowsing, which captured her heart for many years. But she also trained in several other healing and transformational techniques, consulted with clients, taught and then ended up working with spiritual entrepreneurs.

At the time of this writing, she is not sure she has found the one thing she will do that will be her last career choice. We live in a time of rapid spiritual evolution, and many people have apparently chosen the path of learning many things to help them on their spiritual journey while helping others.

Your Main Purpose Is To Be Fulfilled And Happy

Whatever you choose to do with your life, the important thing is that it allows you to experience joy. When you find what makes your heart sing, stick with that. Don't allow yourself to be trapped in a dead-end job or meaningless career just for money. And don't substitute someone else's values for your own.

Everyone has gifts, and everyone has the potential to use those gifts and be fulfilled. Doing that contributes a great deal to your sense of happiness. You know in your heart whether you are happy doing what you now do. If you are unfulfilled and unhappy, definitely take action to get yourself closer to what makes you happy.

Meanwhile, although you can probably 'know' without dowsing, here are some questions you can ask using dowsing that will help you think about your life choices.

On a scale of 0 to 10, with 10 being best/smoothest/fastest/easiest, how does my current life situation rank with respect to fulfilling my life's/soul's purpose at this time?

Technically, there are no wrong choices in life. Every choice you make can take you closer to your goals. Some choices may take you on a scenic detour, but you can still get there. Other choices are painful, but you can learn much from them.

The purpose of life is to live. It's that simple. So tune in to your intuition and listen to your heart. You know if you are on the path to a happy, fulfilling life.

〜

All The Career & Life Path Questions

USE this chart to dowse whatever you like and watch progress over time. We include two blanks, so remember to save one for copying...

On all levels of my being, do I believe...

I am good enough to succeed?

It's safe for me to succeed?

The Universe will support me and help me succeed?

My family and loved ones want me to succeed?

I have all the talents I need to succeed?

On any level of my being, do I believe...

Others will reject me if I succeed?

My family will reject me if I succeed?

Others will be jealous of me if I succeed?

I will be killed if I succeed?

Success will ruin my life?

I will not go to heaven if I succeed?

I am only spiritual because I am poor?

On a scale of 0-10, how big an impact is this belief having on my ability to succeed at my goals?

On a scale of 0-10, with 10 being best, how much do I believe on all levels that I have all the talent it takes to succeed at my goals?

On a scale of 0-10, with 10 being best, how much do I agree (on all levels of my being) that I am intelligent enough to achieve my goals?

On a scale of 0-10, with 10 being best, how much am I in alignment on all levels of my being with my goals about my career?

On a scale of 0-10, with 10 being best, how much confidence do I have overall in my ability to achieve my goals?

On a scale of 0-10, with 0 being best, how much energy am I holding at any level that is not in alignment with my current career goals?

Am I currently being negatively affected in my career goals by other lifetimes?

How much on a scale of 10, with 0 being no effect, am I being impacted negatively by other lives at this time in my career goals?

On any level of my being, do I believe I must do what my parents want me to do?

On any level of my being, do I believe that I cannot have what I want?

On any level of my being, do I believe it is selfish for me to do what I want?

On any level of my being, do I doubt that I have enough talent to successfully express my gift?

On any level of my being, do I believe I cannot support myself with my gift?

On any level of my being, do I believe I will be rejected if I live my passion?

On any level of my being, do I fear the judgment of my family for living my passion?

On any level of my being, do I believe that I will attract jealousy from those close to me if I express my gift?

On any level of my being, do I fear the results of expressing my gift?

On any level of my being, do I feel I have to let others dictate what I do?

At the subconscious level, do I believe that expressing my gift will cause others to reject me?

At the subconscious level, do I believe my gift is valuable?

At the subconscious level, do I believe that following my passion and expressing my gift can support me financially?

At the subconscious level, am I afraid of what others will think if I express my gift and live my passion?

At the subconscious level, do I have any blocks to expressing my gift and living my passion?

At the subconscious level, do I have fear about the effects of expressing my gift and living my passion?

On all levels, do I feel competent to support myself by living my passion?

Do I believe on any level of my being that I cannot make a living doing what I love?

Do I believe on any level of my being that my gift is not valuable enough to sell it?

Am I expressing at any level family beliefs or patterns that say you can't succeed by doing what you love?

On all levels, do I accept that I am gifted?

On all levels, am I willing to accept that my talent exists and can help lots of people?

On all levels, am I willing to acknowledge my gifts?

Am I afraid to accept that I am gifted?

Do I fear negative consequences if I know what my gifts are?

Am I afraid that I will have to do something I don't want to if I acknowledge my gifts?

Do I feel safer ignoring my gifts than accepting and using them?

On a scale of +10 to -10, with positive numbers being good results, what is the overall level in effects for my goals of applying for _____(name the job)?

On a scale of +10 to -10, with positive numbers being good results, how happy would I be in _____(name a time, like 5 years) if I accept the job and the current terms offered, considering my goals?

On a scale of 0 to 10, with 10 being best/smoothest/fastest/easiest, how does my current life situation rank with respect to fulfilling my life's/soul's purpose at this time?

Dowsing Deeper

DOWSING ISN'T THE END...

Dowsing is a powerful tool. It's part of your natural array of intuitive senses. The more you dowse, especially if you dowse the 'right' way, the more you tune in to your other intuitive senses. You get useful information that can really make a difference in your life.

Focusing only on the movement of a tool or feeling that you are getting answers from some outside source will not empower you to expand your intuitive sensing abilities. Listening to your Inner Voice, noticing how your body feels when you dowse and allowing yourself to 'see' things will connect you to other intuitive abilities that will take you beyond dowsing.

At some point, most dowsers start 'getting' the answers before their tool shows an answer. This is a sign that you have developed your sensing ability beyond basic dowsing. Don't mistrust it. Go with it. Confirm it. Lose the tool. Begin to use all your intuitive senses and life will become richer and happier.

LIFE CHANGES, And So Should You

The energies we live in are much different from those in the past. In the past, the energies often supported the status quo, making change difficult. Now, the energy of change is powerful and impossible to ignore. Or if you do fight it, you do so at your peril.

"Going with the flow" was never more important. This era is about the evolution of humanity. We are thinking in new ways, changing our values, expressing ourselves differently. What started as a fringe movement is now spreading into the conventional sector, affecting such mundane, ordinary things as marketing.

Maybe in the past it was sensible for people to value how they did not change from year to year, how they were totally predictable no matter what. But that isn't the case now. Our culture is evolving, and there is great opportunity for personal growth. But that means letting go of old paradigms that no longer serve you. Sometimes that is difficult. Dowsing can be very empowering, and thus can lead you to have more confidence about being authentically you.

Listening To Your Heart

Dowsing is ultimately a way to listen to your heart. Our culture doesn't always value that. But your heart does not lead you wrong.

By 'heart' we mean your innermost 'knowing' of what you came here to experience, who you really are. So often we deny that truth because of wanting to please our family, our spouses or our bosses that we live a numb, unrewarding life.

Maggie says: Dowsing was the gateway to listening to my heart, and I'm pretty sure it can do the same thing for you. I had to make a bunch of big changes in my world. All the inauthentic things had to be dropped. People no longer wanted to be around me. Other people were drawn to support me. I found my passion for doing something that made a difference to me and others.

It's always best to listen to your heart, even if it means giving up things that you thought you couldn't do without. Because in the end, you can't live the life you came here to live if you don't follow your heart.

6

RELATIONSHIP QUESTIONS

Overview

The Value Of Happiness...

Perhaps nowhere do people link success and happiness more than in matters of relationships. Perhaps that is because relationships revolve around love, and love and happiness are often intertwined.

Relationships matter. And using dowsing to focus on your heart and use your intuition will help you make better relationship choices than if you only use your head. And that will lead to greater happiness.

By using your heart, we don't mean making decisions based on infatuation or wishful thinking or even on strong emotions. We mean listen to the wisdom of your heart, and be guided by what it tells you.

The message may not always be welcome, but if you follow your inner guidance, your life will certainly be happier.

Detachment Is Vital

Any time you dowse, detachment is needed if you want an accurate answer. Yet it can be very hard to be detached if you have a preconceived attitude. Remember when you were very young, and you would pull the petals off daisies and say, "He loves me; he loves me not", wondering which statement it would end on? Or when you were older, you consulted a psychic to see what she would say about your latest lover? Or, if you are more left-brain dominant, you might have studied personality theory or even astrology to understand the attraction or problems in your relationships.

There's nothing wrong with doing any of the above, but you don't need to if you are an accurate dowser. Dowsing allows you to tune in to the energies and flow of a situation, a person or a decision. You focus on your question and then let go. The answer comes to you, and you act on it.

If you feel fear or the attachment to a certain answer when dowsing, your answer will probably be wrong. The best thing to do is practice dowsing every day so that you become detached and able to accept the answers, whatever they are. After all, what will be, will be, and knowing what's best for you puts an advantage in your hands.

Be Willing To Be Surprised

The best attitude a dowser can cultivate is curiosity. If you are able to allow yourself to be open to surprising answers, to answers you would not have predicted, you are probably a good dowser. And when you act on those answers that go against what you expected, because they 'feel' so right, you will be blessed with positive outcomes.

This is a process that takes time. Don't rush it. You won't be able to be detached about all things or right away, but with practice, you will find yourself rewarded with insights and answers that make your life flow smoother, and you will be so grateful you took up dowsing.

~

Evaluating Blocks To Happy Relationships

Compatibility Questions

Compatibility is a predictor of relationship success. There is no one right type of compatibility. Sometimes, opposites attract, then lead to disaster. Other times, similarities breed not boredom, but peace and contentment.

If you are unusual in that you know yourself very well and with complete honesty, you know what type of person who best suits you in a long term relationship, or a short one. But most people haven't analyzed themselves or their attractions to other people in enough depth to have this information. They simply respond to the emotions that are kindled by an interaction and follow where they lead.

Dowsing allows you to predict how well any type of relationship will turn out based on compatibility and your values and goals in the relationship.

A word of caution: you can dowse what your significant other or date or friend thinks or feels or intends. But you would do better to confront the person directly and ask. If you don't feel you can communicate with someone, you don't have much chance of a successful relationship. If they can't or won't tell you the truth, the relationship is probably doomed anyway. **So don't use dowsing as an excuse not to talk or ask someone a direct question. Poor or no communication is the cause of almost all the relationship problems you see.**

As with all types of dowsing, we advise you to make a list of goals and values and be sure to define your terms very clearly. Each person will be different.

There are many types of relationships: friend, lover, marriage partner, business partner. In each, you will have specific goals and values. Some people will place honesty and loyalty high on the list of what they need or want. Others might care more about how fun-loving and intelligent a partner or friend is going to be. Respect, thoughtfulness, kindness, gentleness, fidelity, openness: these are just some of the traits that might matter to you.

Any trait you feel is a deal breaker, please put it on the list and say so out loud. Set your intention to get a negative number if the person ranks below a _____(an 8 or whatever number you choose as the cutoff) on a scale of 10, with 10 being the best.

Then dowse the question:

On a scale of +10 to -10, with positive numbers indicating a positive outcome, how does _____(name of person) rank in terms of compatibility as a_____(type of relationship) for me at this time, considering my values and goals?

Another tack you can take (instead of asking the same question twice, which is never a good idea, is to check the long term effects of a relationship decision, if you are wanting long term happiness:

On a scale of +10 to -10, with positive numbers indicating happiness and success, what are the long term effects of _____(name of person) as a _____(type of relationship) for me, with long term being _____(name a length of time)?

Another way to ask:

If I were to choose _____(name of person) as a _____(type of relationship), how happy would I be in_____(length of time from now) on a scale of +10 to -10, with positive numbers indicating happiness?

Relationship Troubles & How To Understand Them

LOVE & Attraction: Karmic Relationships

People whom you have the biggest challenges with or the most attraction to are in your life for a reason. Huge, unexplainable attraction is usually the work of a karmic relationship. A karmic relationship could indicate you and the person to whom you are attracted have unfinished business, good or bad, from another lifetime. Thus you are drawn to each other for the chance of resolving it.

On some occasions a karmic relationship is an attraction to someone you are meant to be with, for good or bad, as part of your life's path this time around.

A strong attraction to a person does NOT necessarily mean you will be happy with that person. Often it means just the opposite. All the attraction means is that you are drawn to be with that person, for good or ill.

Because you can't tell the root cause of a karmic relationship easily, dowsing is a very useful tool. Maggie was able to tell that her attraction to Nigel very early in their relationship was a result of them belonging together in this life as life partners. She also found that they had experienced many lives together, some happy, some sad, and that this lifetime would be a chance to resolve some unresolved issues from those lifetimes.

When you have a strong attraction to a person, it is wise to dowse the compatibility and happiness questions, because that attraction will eventually open the door to whatever else is coming, and dowsing will help you see what that is and make a choice that is best for you.

People Who Drive You Crazy

Some people in your life just make your life hard. They betray; they ignore; they criticize. Often these people will be people you can't easily escape, or think you can't. They might be family or co-workers or a boss. You find yourself forced to deal with them, even though it's always tough.

The people in your life who are the biggest challenges are there to help you learn about yourself. Their most annoying trait reveals your inner judgment and fears. This process is called 'projection', during which that trait or attitude you most dislike in yourself becomes thrown onto another person and highlighted, giving you a chance to rethink your judgment and attitude or beliefs.

If instead of reacting negatively to the most challenging people you meet, you learn to ask yourself how are they projections of your own traits, issues and beliefs that you would rather not admit, then you have the opportunity to shift some energy and change the pattern.

Here's an example: You have a pattern of being dis-respected by people in spite of being a diligent worker, a thoughtful friend and a loyal family member. Your boss constantly treats you like you are an idiot, even making fun of you in front of others. Why? Well, yes, he's a jerk, but metaphysically, this is an opportunity for you to grow.

If you understand that his actions are a reflection of your greatest fears, beliefs, and attitudes, then you will understand that he dis-respects you because you dis-respect yourself. You don't feel you have any inherent value. You don't love and accept yourself. You never support yourself or feel deserving. If you address your issues, you will find you no longer attract disrespectful people.

Dowsing will help you discover your subconscious beliefs that are leading to problems in relationships so you can clear or transform those energies. The next section shows you how.

YOUR SUBCONSCIOUS ISSUES & Beliefs

Our lives are run by our subconscious. You think you know what you believe, but that's only what you consciously believe, and no one lives consciously for very long or very often.

Your subconscious holds the key to your life experiences, and dowsing will help reveal your relationship issues so you can do something about them. We include your relationship and view of yourself. That's because loving yourself is the biggest part of attracting love, and most people are not able to love themselves well.

You can dowse:

On the subconscious level, do I believe I deserve to be happy in my relationships (or name a particular type)?

On the subconscious level, do I believe I am able to achieve happiness/success/joy in _____(name the type of relationship and the person as appropriate)?

On the subconscious level, do I want to be successful/happy in _____(name the type of relationship and the person, as appropriate)?

On the subconscious level, do I totally love and accept myself as I am?

On the subconscious level, do I believe I must judge myself?

On the subconscious level, do I believe I have inherent value?

On the subconscious level, do I feel worthy of being loved?

On the subconscious level, do I believe my relationships must have conflict?

On the subconscious level, do I equate conflict with love?

On the subconscious level, do I believe I must be rejected by those I love?

On the subconscious level, do I believe I must be judged by those I love?

On the subconscious level, am I afraid of committing to a loving relationship?

On the subconscious level, do I equate fighting with love?

There are an endless variety of questions you can dowse. If you observe the patterns in your life that you would like to change, but haven't been able to, form a question to test your subconscious and don't be surprised to find out that your subconscious is creating a situation you do not consciously want.

Use whatever clearing method dowses best or feels best for clearing or transforming the energies of faulty beliefs you discover. Then retest the beliefs and see if they are cleared. It is beyond the scope of this book to talk about all the many clearing techniques available. All focus your intention. You can use color, sound, symbols, prayer, EFT, The Emotion Code, flower essences, essential oils or whatever clearing method you are most attracted to.

Note that sometimes it takes a little time for a heavy belief to clear, so you might want to retest the belief for three days after the clearing to see if it is gone. In most cases, it will be if you chose the right clearing method.

∽

Relationship Choices

Use A Balanced Approach

Relationships often end badly for one or both parties. There is always a lesson to learn, no matter how unpleasant the situation. But would you like to learn life lessons without it being painful? Wouldn't it be wonderful if making good relationship choices taught you confidence and trust?

This may seem obvious, but using both your heart and your head in proper measure gives the best results in relationships. By heart, we mean your intuition, not your infatuation, lust or desire for romance. By head, we mean the logical part of your mind.

Karmic Relationship Choices

In an earlier section we pointed out that some attractions are amazingly strong. They often indicate either a very positive karmic energy or a very negative one. In both cases, you are strongly attracted to the relationship, because engaging in it will give you a chance to resolve a big issue that's been following you around for many lifetimes.

Karmic relationships that tend to have negative consequences are those that put you in a similar position to past lives and offer you a chance to make a different, better choice.

An example would be marrying someone who is abusive and violent, and doing something to have the outcome differ from in the past. In the past, you may have been a victim many times over, and this time, you could walk away or get the person arrested for bad behavior. The abuser also is in a karmic situation, as he or she could choose not to be abusive this time around.

Sadly, it is very challenging to create a different outcome, so we think it's really best to avoid those relationships. If you are in one, the best thing you can do is identify the pattern you are being offered to break, and find a safe, legal and quick way to break it and move on.

Other occasions, you may be drawn to someone who is here to be a very big supporter to you in this life. Such relationships may have their challenges, but offer a great reward.

Here are some questions you can dowse if you feel you are involved in a karmic relationship:

On a scale of +10 to -10, what is the OVERALL long term level in effects on my health, well-being and happiness of entering and staying in a _____(type of relationship) with _____(name of person) at this time?

Note you are asking long term effects. You can substitute other things to measure, like financial well-being, mental health, whatever matters to you. If you get a negative number, run the other way. If you get a positive number, that's good. But as always, we recommend +8 or higher be the cutoff point for any major action you take. You want big returns for an investment this large.

This is definitely a subject where you would not want to use the phrase "highest and greatest good" as a measure of what to do. Why not? If at any level, you believe that learning a very hard and painful lesson is a good thing overall, you might dowse to marry an abusive spouse or enter into a partnership where you will be betrayed. So don't use vague terms or phrases.

If you are curious, you can ask about past lives with this person. See the section on that subject in a later chapter. Knowing the 'history' sometimes helps you to make a clear decision.

MARRIAGE

This section not only relates to marriage, but to any anticipated long-term intimate relationship, with or without religious or legal blessing.

Since so many marriages end in divorce, it makes sense to make the wisest choice you can. Combining both intuition and logic is very helpful. Put aside emotions like fear or infatuation, as they cloud your ability to make good decisions.

Dowsing can help you connect with your intuition and make better choices. As with all important choices, we urge you to get a second and third opinion.

Note however, that in some cases (a minority), you may find yourself alone with no outside support about the decision you want to make. If that happens, you must be in touch with your intuition very clearly and follow it no matter what.

If you have been practicing and using dowsing, you will be at a big advantage if you are ever in this situation, as Maggie was when she first knew Nigel.

Each person has his or her own goals when entering a marriage, so it is important to take time to list your goals before you dowse. Make sure you have included everything that is important to you.

Once you have a complete list, you may dowse:

Considering all my goals, what is the overall level in effects on me of entering into marriage with _____(name of person) at this time?

Don't do anything that gives a negative number. Go for +8 or higher before taking action.

You might have some other questions you'd like to ask:

On a scale of 0-10, with 10 being excellent, how good would _____(name of person) be for me as a life partner at this time in this life?

8 or higher is the best score. Be sure you define what you mean by 'life partner'.

DIVORCE

No one enters into a marriage planning a divorce. Yet so many marriages end in divorce. Part of the reason is that at this time, many people have chosen before incarnating to have the opportunity to resolve lots of old issues from other lives with various people, and having a number of marriages allows for this.

If you have gone through divorce, don't beat yourself up. Learn from the experience and move on. It's an opportunity. Don't repeat patterns that create sadness or victimhood.

At some point in most people's lives, they have to make a choice about staying in a relationship or going. Often they have considered leaving for many years, but it seems impossible. The penalties financially and socially are quite high. And no one really wants to abandon their children (well, most don't).

The bottom line is, if you are unhappy in a relationship or there is violence or misery, you are not giving your children good example of what marriage is, and they will marry someone who helps them recreate the negative dynamics. You owe it to them to take appropriate action to protect yourself, them and your happiness.

Dowsing can be a valuable tool in helping you to make a serious choice like this. As with all major life choices, it hinges on your goals. If financial security matters most to you, then you probably won't get a good dowsing response for divorce. If happiness is your priority, you may get a very high number.

More than likely you have several goals. Make a list and prioritize them. Then dowse:

Considering all of my goals, what is the overall long term level in effects for me on a scale of +10 to -10, with positive numbers meaning a positive outcome, of divorcing _____(name spouse) at this time?

You can replace the wording if you are not legally married and just ask about leaving the relationship.

You can also change the time and check some near future dates, if you don't get a positive answer for right now.

Note: You don't need to dowse about the effects on spouse or children if your goal is health and happiness, because whatever is best for you is also best in the long run for them using those criteria. If however, your goals are material, then you might want to dowse the same question to find the effects on them, because the answers might be different.

To reiterate: if you only care about money and security, that is a selfish goal, but it may be your honest one. If you are seeking true health and happiness, then whatever fulfills you will fulfill your family in the long run, whether they realize it or not.

PARTNERSHIPS

A business partnership is very much like a marriage, and a business breakup is like a divorce.

Dowsing can be very useful when you are considering entering into a partnership or leaving one. As always, you should list your specific goals for entering this partnership or leaving it, because the answer may vary depending on different goals.

Once you have a list of goals, then dowse the question:

Considering my goals, on a scale of +10 to -10, with positive numbers indicating a positive outcome, what is the long term overall level in effects of entering into _____(type of partnership) with _____(name) at this time (or pick whatever time you want to test)?

Considering my goals, on a scale of +10 to -10, with positive numbers indicating positive outcomes, what is the long term overall level in effects of leaving my partnership (or use the appropriate term) with _____(name of person or company) at this time (or put the time in that you want to test)?

OTHER USEFUL TECHNIQUES

A +8 or higher is likely to give you the best outcome. As with all questions, you can ask the question about each individual item in your goal list. You can then identify which areas are weaker and which are stronger.

So instead of "considering my goals", you'd dowse "considering his/her honesty" or "considering my financial security" or "considering my mental health". One really low number will pull the average down, and if it is an important item, great. But if it was a lesser item, remove it from the list and see what the overall score then becomes.

We are not suggesting you water down your goals, but it is wise to see where the strengths and weaknesses are. Hopefully you know yourself well enough to know what is a deal-breaker.

Dowsing the individual items in your goal list can help you make a better decision. For example, to most people, honesty and trust is hugely important in a relationship. If a marriage with someone tests low for honesty, that might be enough to refuse the offer. Same for business partnerships.

Definitions matter. If you put "communicates well" and that subject made the marriage test as poor, then maybe you need to break that subject down a bit more. If someone is introverted, they might not easily open up with you, but that doesn't mean they are dishonest or would try to hide things.

~

All The Relationship Questions

USE this chart to dowse whatever you like and watch progress over time. We include two blanks, so remember to save one for copying...

On a scale of +10 to -10, with positive numbers indicating a positive outcome, how does _____(name of person) rank in terms of compatibility as a_____(type of relationship) for me at this time, considering my values and goals?

On a scale of +10 to -10, with positive numbers indicating happiness and success, what are the long term effects of _____(name of person) as a _____(type of relationship) for me, with long term being _____(name a length of time)?

If I were to choose _____(name of person) as a _____(type of relationship), how happy would I be in_____(length of time from now) on a scale of +10 to -10, with positive numbers indicating happiness?

On the subconscious level, do I believe I deserve to be happy in my relationships (or name a particular type)?

On the subconscious level, do I believe I am able to achieve happiness/success/joy in _____(name the type of relationship and the person as appropriate)?

On the subconscious level, do I want to be successful/happy in
_____(name the type of relationship and the person, as
appropriate)?

On the subconscious level, do I totally love and accept myself as I am?

On the subconscious level, do I believe I must judge myself?

On the subconscious level, do I believe I have inherent value?

On the subconscious level, do I feel worthy of being loved?

On the subconscious level, do I believe my relationships must have
conflict?

On the subconscious level, do I equate conflict with love?

On the subconscious level, do I believe I must be rejected by those
I love?

On the subconscious level, do I believe I must be judged by those
I love?

On the subconscious level, am I afraid of committing to a loving
relationship?

On the subconscious level, do I equate fighting with love?

On a scale of +10 to -10, what is the OVERALL long term level in
effects on my health, well-being and happiness of entering and staying
in a _____(type of relationship) with
_____(name of person) at this time?

Considering all my goals, what is the overall level in effects on me of
entering into marriage with _____(name of person) at
this time?

On a scale of 0-10, with 10 being excellent, how good would
_____(name of person) be for me as a life partner at this
time in this life?

Considering all of my goals, what is the overall long term level in effects for me on a scale of +10 to -10, with positive numbers meaning a positive outcome, of divorcing _____(name spouse) at this time?

Considering my goals, on a scale of +10 to -10, with positive numbers indicating a positive outcome, what is the long term overall level in effects of entering into _____(type of partnership) with _____(name) at this time (or pick whatever time you want to test)?

Considering my goals, on a scale of +10 to -10, with positive numbers indicating positive outcomes, what is the long term overall level in effects of leaving my partnership (or use the appropriate term) with _____(name of person or company) at this time (or put the time in that you want to test)?

~

Dowsing Deeper

THE IMPORTANCE Of Knowing Your Goals

In Western culture, we are too inclined to be swept away by infatuation and feelings of romance that rarely indicate long-term relationship success. In other cultures, where marriages are arranged, people's emotions are not given any importance at all. The best course is balanced in between the two.

Your intuition is powerful, and your heart will tell you the truth about any relationship if you let it. Often, you won't want to listen to what it is saying, because it is cautioning you to go slower, or even to run the other way. And when you meet someone from another lifetime who represents a karmic relationship, it can be very, very hard not to throw yourself into the relationship, even when it's obviously doomed. Even when everyone tells you it's a mistake.

Your best bet is to use your rational mind and be very clear about your relationship goals. Then tune into your heart with your intuitive senses and ask what the probable outcome is in terms of your goals if you pursue this relationship. Try to be detached and curious and allow the answer to come through.

You can still choose to make your life miserable, but at least you will have actually chosen, instead of being swept along and overpowered by self-destructive or foolish desires. Dowsing can help you with this process, and if you are an accurate dowser and follow your answers, you will avoid much pain and sadness.

OVERALL VS. SPECIFIC Answers

An overall rating of something like a potential relationship is a good starting point. But often there are one or two specific factors that are deal breakers. And they aren't the same for everyone. Some women won't have anything to do with a philanderer. Some men require loyalty and honesty of their partners, and those terms can be defined in different ways.

If you want to dive deeper into dowsing about relationships, this is a good subject for breaking down the question into its specific parts. By asking the question about each factor, you can find where the potential incompatibilities and disappointments lie.

For example, if you asked about the compatibility of you and _____ on a scale of +10 to -10, and you got a 7, and you were attracted to the person, you'd probably want to justify going with a 7, even though we generally say only go with decisions that give 8 or higher.

This is an important decision. So you can break down the question and find out what each factor rated. Although the average was 7, there could be a 10 and a 4, and don't you think it would be good to know which is which?

By asking about every specific factor that matters to you, you can see the strengths and weaknesses of the relationship. If the lower numbers are about factors you can live with, great. If they are in key factors you really want an 8 or higher in, then you know you are headed for trouble if you proceed with the relationship.

We wish we'd had this tool when we were younger, as it might have saved us a lot of trouble.

CHECKING Your Answer

How are you supposed to do that, you ask? If you turn down a marriage proposal, how will you know it was a good choice? The thing about choices is that you don't always get confirmation of your results. We suggest you ask the Universe for confirmation of your answers so that you can see that you made a good choice.

If's easy if you followed the dowsing that said the relationship would be good. You'll be able to see whether you were right or not. If it appears you were not right, re-examine your goals. Did you leave something off the list? That happens. You forgot to include honesty, and your spouse is dishonest, and you can't stand it. Well, you just got confirmation.

What if you decide NOT to have a relationship or partnership based on dowsing? How can you tell if it was the right thing? As time passes, if you allow yourself to be in touch with your heart, your intuition will let you know you made the right choice. And you will find someone who makes you happy, and that will further confirm your choice.

GOING AGAINST YOUR FAMILY & Friends

Nowhere will you find this a factor more often than in relationship choices. Some people feel strongly against divorce for religious or social reasons. Others are against marrying certain types of people. Many are prejudiced against same sex relationships.

If you find yourself having to make a choice about a relationship, and your friends and family are all or mostly against it, there are two possibilities. Either they are right in predicting you will be sorry, or they are wrong. But it's your choice, and you need to do what's right for you.

You might think that if someone is against your loved one because of race or religion, then that makes their opinion invalid. What it does is make the reason behind their opinion invalid. Maybe their opinion is correct. Maybe they have a feeling about the person and don't know why, so they grasp at whatever makes sense to them.

On the other hand, people who selfishly judge someone based on shallow things often misjudge them. This isn't about how bigoted you parents are or how valid their opinions are. It's about you using your head and your heart to make a good decision for yourself.

It is important not to give your power to others. Using dowsing will help you gain confidence in making good choices that will bring you long term success, and it will teach you to stick with those choices and have confidence in them. I

It is wise to listen to what others who love you have to say, but in the end, you are the one who will have to live with your choice. So make the choice you believe in.

Dowsing will help you make a happier choice. Sometimes that means going against what everyone thinks. But not always.

Following Your Dowsing

This can be hard to do when you dowse things like it would be an 8 out of 10 for you to get divorced or split up with your business partner of 10 years.

Sometimes, doing the dowsing is the easy part. Following through is the hard part. If you get a dowsing answer that you feel fearful about implementing, ask the Universe to give you a sign that the answer is correct, and to send you help to have all the resources you need to make it easy to follow through on that choice.

Always get a second and even a third opinion before taking action, but be sure you are asking dowsers you trust completely, and use blind dowsing as appropriate to help them stay detached.

There Are No Mistakes

Whatever you choose to do, it isn't about being wrong or right. Every choice gives you a chance to learn, grow and experience. Sometimes the experience isn't much fun, but it can teach you something very valuable about yourself. Sometimes the experience is heavenly. But whatever you choose to do, you can benefit from the experience, so don't regard it as a right or wrong choice.

Dowsing is a real benefit at times like this. Being able to really know what you feel; being in touch with your heart are things that dowsing help you do, and when you have a choice to make in a relationship, and you have powerful emotions tugging at you, the time you have spent dowsing will help you get in touch with your heart. You will find it easier to sense if your 'love' is infatuation or real. You will be able to tell if your heart is saying, "Don't go there!".

We have found that becoming a dowser can really expand all your intuitive sensing capabilities, and that helps you make better choices across the board in life.

7

FINANCIAL QUESTIONS

Overview

Use Your Head...

Don't use dowsing as an excuse to make poor financial choices. Dowsing can help you learn to release fears and judgments about money. It will help you tap into your natural intuitive ability, so that you can reach your financial goals. But the process takes time.

Money issues are one of the most common blocks in the world. Just look around. How many people are comfortable financially? Not a huge percentage of the population. Lack and poverty are the rule.

The suggestions in this book are not meant to replace common sense choices. Instead, they are aimed at helping you release poverty energy and align yourself with whatever financial goals you have.

Don't spend money you don't have. Don't run up credit card debt. Use this book to help manifest not only what you need to survive, but to create a lifestyle you can enjoy.

·   ·   ·

Be Patient

Change takes time. Especially if a habit or pattern has been lifelong, don't expect it to change overnight. And as you may be aware, healing comes in layers. Give yourself permission to have a pleasant healing process. Don't push for overnight success.

Measure Progress Sensibly

Evaluate your progress not by how you feel on a given day. Think about how you are reacting to situations now compared to how you did a year ago. Note how much your fear has been reduced concerning money issues.

Focus on evaluating how much more positive and proactive you are acting compared to a year ago. Ask yourself how would you have reacted to this situation last year, and then say how grateful you are for the changes.

Don't look at what hasn't changed. Don't focus on what needs to change. Look at what HAS changed. Express gratitude. Build confidence that change will continue.

~

Evaluating Your Blocks To Abundance

You Don't Want To Be Wealthy...

No, you don't. If you aren't wealthy, then no matter what you may think, you aren't aligned with wealth. If you align with abundance, you experience it. It's as simple as that.

The secret is to realize that your subconscious is in control of your life experience, and that is the biggest factor in your challenges to reaching your financial goals.

In this chapter, we will show you how to use dowsing to uncover the blocks that have been holding you back and how to find the best way of clearing them.

Find Out What Your Subconscious Believes

In this section, you can use dowsing to have a dialogue with your subconscious and find out what it believes. Then you can decide if you want to get your subconscious in alignment with your conscious goals and find out what will best do that.

It's important to remember a detached and curious attitude is required for accuracy. Do NOT be afraid to hear the truth. Do NOT judge yourself for having 'stupid' beliefs. We all do. Get over it. Just be grateful that you have dowsing, the best and easiest way to find out what your subconscious believes.

Note that we are using 'rich', 'wealthy' and 'financial abundance' interchangeably for these questions.

At the subconscious level, I want to experience financial abundance now.

At the subconscious level, I believe it is safe to experience financial abundance now and on an ongoing basis.

At the subconscious level, I believe that wealthy people are greedy.

At the subconscious level, I believe that being poor is more spiritual than being rich.

At the subconscious level, I believe it is possible for me to be wealthy at this time.

At the subconscious level, I believe that being rich will cause people to be jealous of me.

At the subconscious level, I believe that being rich will keep me from entering heaven.

At the subconscious level, I feel that being poor is morally superior to being rich.

Note that there are a number of subject areas that these questions fall into. You can add further questions when you see which patterns are strongest in your life:

◆Religious beliefs that say wealth makes you less spiritual and less likely to get into heaven

◆Social beliefs that say others won't like you if you are rich

◆Personal concerns about safety that say rich people get kidnaped, are targets of burglary and con men

◆Feelings that the government or powers that be will just take away wealth if you get it; you can't keep it without breaking the law or hiding it

◆Fear that you will lose friends and family if you become rich and they are not

◆Poverty consciousness often stems from a sense of victimhood and powerlessness. If you have a lot of those energies, it will be very tough to become wealthy

◆If you judge or envy successful rich people instead of having rich role models you admire, you will find it harder to be wealthy.

Many of these subject areas are easy to identify without dowsing. You know how you feel. You know what type of things you say and post on Facebook. If you are talking negatively about the rich, you aren't going to be rich. If you think rich people are jerks, you will never be rich (unless you're a jerk).

WHAT YOU EXPERIENCE Is What You Resonate With

Dowsing is the fastest and easiest way to find out your subconscious blocks, but you can also learn about them by observing your life experience and making some sharp conclusions about what they indicate about your energy.

Make a list of what you believe about rich people, wealth and abundance. If it's mostly negative, you need to shift that.

Make a list of what you feel about yourself and your ability to create abundance. If you don't feel powerful, that needs to change.

Make a list of the past experiences you have had that you consider will or might repeat. Note how most of them are negative.

Observe how you tend to predict your future based on your past, and that isn't always a very positive thing.

Notice how often you expect bad things to happen, but how rarely you expect pleasant surprises, yet both are equally likely in life.

Observe the types of people you hang out with. What is their income? What are their attitudes? You can tell what your beliefs are by observing your closest friends and associates.

If you are complaining, blaming and justifying, you are solidifying the status quo. Is the status quo what you want? If not, then start focusing on what you want to create and find ways to take action towards making it happen.

CLEARING Blocks

This book is not about clearing methods, so we won't go into a lot of detail. There are many wonderful, effective methods for clearing energy blocks and for aligning with your conscious goals. Where dowsing comes in best is in choosing what will be most effective for you.

Remember that you are changing, and a method that works great now may not work great in a year. Also, what works for one block might be less effective for another. Have a number of tools in your tool kit and dowse which one is best for a given situation.

Some examples of tools include: color, symbols, statements of intention, crystals, essential oils, flower essences, EFT (Emotional Freedom Technique), SRT (Spiritual Response Therapy), Senzar Clearing, The Emotion Code, The Healing Codes and many other therapies and techniques.

On a scale of 0 to 10, with 0 being no effect and 10 being the greatest positive effect, how effective would _____(insert method) be for clearing _____(name the block) quickly, easily, comfortably and with no negative side effects at this time?

For best results, how long would I need to apply/use _____(insert method) in order to permanently clear that block at that level?

For best results, how often would I need to apply/use_____(insert method) in order to permanently clear that block at that level?

∼

Investing

Don't Gamble!

Many forms of investment are simply ways to gamble your money away. Do not invest any money you cannot afford to lose. Don't assume you will get the results promised. Do your due diligence and only invest when you feel you have checked everything out carefully.

Dowsing is not meant to be a short cut to doing the work necessary to make wise investments. Don't be stupid! Dowsing can help you evaluate an opportunity. It will help you get in touch with your intuition and heart.

Use dowsing as an additional tool to make wise investment decisions.

Get a second or third opinion wherever possible. Use blind dowsing as needed to help you detach from your personal bias.

DOWSING About Investments

Investments can be anything from a stock to a business opportunity to an offer from a relative about joining a partnership to invest in something.

List the priorities you have for a positive outcome. What percent return do you want as a minimum in a certain time period? How much are you willing to invest? How much say do you want in the process, if this includes participation? How much is the partner or venture in alignment with your values? What level of integrity do you desire in the partners or business or stock you invest in?

Once you are clear on the priorities, you can dowse.

On a scale of +10 to -10, with negative numbers being a bad outcome for my stated goals and priorities, what is the overall level in effects over the next _____(list a time period, like one year-as appropriate) of investing _____(amount of money or resources) with _____(list the stock or business or partner) at this time?

Do not participate in a venture that gives a negative number. However, you can go back and look at your stated goals and make sure you have stated them clearly and not left anything out. It is best not to invest in anything that gives less than a +8 overall.

If there is a particular issue that is paramount to you, you can ask about that one item to make sure it is a high positive number. Be sure you have clearly defined the terms.

On a scale of +10 to -10, what is the level of honesty and integrity in _____(the company or person) about this business venture/opportunity for me?

• • •

Always Follow Your Intuition...

It can be very hard to do this, especially if others are involved, and they disagree with you. But you have to learn when your intuition is saying, "Don't do that" and listen to it, no matter what. You do need to distinguish between fear and a 'bad intuition' about something. Fear or resistance is not a reason to avoid investing. A strong negative hunch or intuition is worth listening to.

Here's an example from our lives:

We always dowse about any big investment for our business. Early in our career of establishing ourselves on the internet, we invested in consulting with someone who was considered an expert. He was someone of great integrity. He made an honest suggestion that we invest $10,000 to work with someone of his acquaintance who offered what we needed. He was not close to the person, but had only heard positive things.

So, we had a recommendation by someone we trusted. But we dowsed about it anyway and did our due diligence. Maggie came up with a negative number. She also had a bad feeling about the person after looking at her website and had some concerns about the way the woman did business. Nigel, on the other hand, had no such feeling, and his dowsing gave a positive number for working with her.

Because two other people she respected disagreed with her, Maggie put aside her concerns and the money was invested. Within a couple of weeks it became obvious that there was a problem. When we asked for our money back, we were only able to get half of it, with a promise to return an additional $2K over a period of about 10 months. We got absolutely nothing for the $3K, and only $1K of the promised $2K refund ever came through. While our consultant ejected that person's business from his recommendation list, it didn't get our money back.

The lesson is, listen to your intuition. It's better to stand your ground than to give in when you feel you are correct, just because you are in a minority.

Getting Help

How's Your Money Energy?

If your financial situation is in crisis, there is a lot you can do. First of all, you need to work on balancing your energy around money. This is the most important thing you can do. You can dowse how aligned you are with certain ideas and outcomes, and then do whatever work tests best to improve that energy.

Here are some examples of things you can dowse. Remember it's important to be detached and not judge the answers. If you are having financial troubles, something is unbalanced. Don't be afraid to have confirmation. Doing this dowsing can help you pinpoint areas that need work, and that can help restore balance.

On a scale of 0 to 10, with 0 being not in alignment at all and 10 being optimally aligned, how aligned am I overall at this time on all levels of my being with being financially secure?

On a scale of 0 to 10, with 0 being not in alignment at all and 10 being optimally aligned, how aligned am I overall at this time on all levels of my being with being financially wealthy?

On a scale of 0 to 10, with 0 being not in alignment at all and 10 being optimally aligned, how aligned am I overall at this time on all levels of my being with quickly resolving my current financial challenges easily?

On a scale of 0 to 10, with 0 being no resonant energy and 10 being the most I can have, how much am I resonating with shame energy on all levels of my being at this time?

On a scale of 0 to 10, with 0 being no resonant energy and 10 being the most I can have, how much am I resonating with self-punishment energy on all levels of my being at this time?

On a scale of 0 to 10, with 0 being none and 10 being the most resonant

*energy I can have, how much am I resonating with powerlessness on all levels
of my being at this time?*

*On a scale of 0 to 10, with 0 being none and 10 being the most resonant
energy I can have, how much am I resonating with victimhood on all levels of
my being at this time?*

It is very common to have the above energies when you are facing a
financial crisis. Even if it is not of your making, you can still feel these
energies, or feel that you SHOULD feel these energies. You feel judged
and ashamed.

The larger the amount of negative energy, the more effect it will show.
Use whatever clearing technique tests best for transforming the above
energies and align with the positive outcome you wish to experience.
See "Clearing Blocks" in the Evaluation section of this chapter for
dowsing questions.

Remember that healing comes in layers, so doing clearing on big issues
one time probably won't resolve them completely. Be patient and peel
the layers off, and notice the progress, because there will be progress.

SOMETIMES YOU NEED **Help**

When you are in financial crisis, it is often wise to seek outside help.
Sometimes you can get into a debt management program. Other times
you may find it advisable to declare bankruptcy. Still other times, it
may be best to get a loan to tide yourself over during the hard times.
Dowsing can help you feel more confident about the choice you make.

As always, if you have a lot of fear and judgment, your dowsing won't
be accurate. Hopefully you have been practicing detachment and just
being curious about what is best for you, so that you can benefit from
dowsing when important decisions come up.

Blind dowsing, explained in the appendix, is a good method to use
when you don't have as much detachment as you would like on a

subject. Always get a second or third opinion when making important decisions.

How About Getting A Loan?

Often, if things haven't gotten too bad, a loan from a friend or family member, or even a home equity loan, might tide you over while you get things balanced.

Obviously it isn't wise to get a loan if you have no clear idea how you can repay it. That just makes things worse. However, if you are in a bind and just trying to bridge a time gap between sources of income, and you are sure the money is coming by a certain time, and you can repay the loan, that might be a good option.

You can't really be sure about exactly how things will go in the future, so dowsing the advisability of getting a loan, and dowsing about the best type of loan to get, is a wise idea.

First, make a list of all the factors that matter to you about this subject. If you want to be sure it won't impact your friendship with the person loaning you money, or you want to make sure the loan you seek has the best terms you can get, include those in the list.

Everyone has their unique values, and you want to take time to think about what matters most to you. When you have all the points listed, you can dowse this question:

On a scale of +10 to -10, with positive numbers indicating a positive outcome based on all the goals I have listed, what is the ranking at this time of getting a _____(type of loan) from _____(source of loan).

For example, you might dowse getting a personal loan from your father. Or getting a home equity loan from the bank.

If you dowse the number is below +8, then you probably ought to explore other options. A negative number definitely means don't do it.

If you have dowsed every option for a loan that you can think of, and you can't find an option that is +8 or higher, then consider the other options listed here.

How About A Debt Consolidation Program?

There are a number of types of programs that will help you get into payment plans for your accumulated debt by bundling it into one payment, or by bundling your debt and negotiating partial payment with all your creditors.

Debt consolidation plans vary. If you have a modest amount of debt, but can't find a good loan option, or if you know you won't be able to repay the loan in a reasonable time, then perhaps you should research debt consolidation. Having one payment can be a lot less stressful than having many. However, you need to do your due diligence. Some programs are legitimate, while others are not a good bet.

Once you have done your due diligence, and after you have listed all your goals for considering a debt consolidation, you can dowse this question:

On a scale of +10 to -10, with positive numbers meaning a positive outcome based on my goals, what is the value to me at this time of entering _____(name of debt consolidation program) and participating exactly as directed by them for as long as directed by them.

Is Debt Management Better For You?

If you have too much debt to easily enroll in a debt consolidation program, you might be advised to enter a debt management program where a company will consolidate your debts and then negotiate partial payment with all your creditors.

This type of option doesn't always work out, especially if you have a lot of creditors and a lot of debt. While theoretically, if you can pay the monthly fee for the time they state, and if they can successfully negotiate acceptance of partial payment to your creditors, you can usually expect to get out of debt in a few to several years. But this positive outcome assumes the creditors will all accept partial payment. There are a lot of 'ifs'.

Your creditors may not want to wait for payment, and they might be concerned you will go bankrupt and not pay anything. Sometimes they sue you, which you have to respond to, and if that happens, you probably will have to declare bankruptcy anyway. So it is wise to dowse about the advisability of getting into such a program, because if you cannot successfully complete it, you have wasted whatever money you have paid into it.

Make a list of your goals for considering this program, then dowse:

On a scale of +10 to -10, with positive numbers indicating a positive outcome for my listed goals, what is the value to me at this time of participating in _____(name of program).

If you don't get at least a +8, it is probably best to explore other options.

BANKRUPTCY?

No one wants or intends to go bankrupt. But our system has measures in place to help you get back on your feet if you find yourself totally overwhelmed by debt.

There are different types of bankruptcies, and you need to do your due diligence on researching what is best for your needs. Do not just go with what your attorney suggests, unless your attorney is someone you know well and trust. A decision about bankruptcy is a big one, and you want to make the best choice.

After doing your due diligence and consulting an attorney, you will have an idea of what you think is the best choice for you. Make a list of

your goals and reasons for thinking about taking this step, then dowse
this question:

*On a scale of +10 to -10, with positive numbers indicating a positive outcome
for my goals, what is the value to me at this time of declaring
_____(type of bankruptcy).*

As always, a +8 or higher number indicates a good outcome. Less than
that means there are some issues.

ARE YOU SABOTAGING YOURSELF?

A lot of people have subconscious beliefs and issues that make it very
hard to come to a clear decision about debt. It is all too common to feel
shame and even seek punishment when you feel you have failed
financially. These beliefs and emotions can make it very hard to get a
good dowsing answer or make a good decision.

You can use dowsing to see how balanced you are about making a
healthy decision on these subjects. If you have beliefs or energies that
do not support just becoming balanced about money, clear them. You
can identify what they are and measure your progress with dowsing.

*On a scale of 0 to 10, with 0 being none and 10 being the most I could have,
how much shame energy do I have at this time about my financial
situation?*

*On a scale of 0 to 10, with 0 being none, how much self-punishment energy do
I currently have active in my system due to my financial situation?*

*Do I believe on any level of my being that I deserve to be punished for my
financial problems?*

*Do I believe on any level of my being that I am powerless to resolve my
financial issues?*

*Do I believe on any level of my being that I must resolve my financial issues
on my own, without outside help?*

Do I believe it is wrong for my debt to be forgiven, and that I must pay every bit back?

There are many other statements you can test, but this will get you started. Use whatever clearing method you know that tests well for balancing your energy and getting rid of false beliefs or sabotage.

All The Financial Questions

Use this chart to dowse whatever you like and watch progress over time. We include two blanks, so remember to save one for copying...

At the subconscious level, I want to experience financial abundance now.

At the subconscious level, I believe it is safe to experience financial abundance now and on an ongoing basis.

At the subconscious level, I believe that wealthy people are greedy.

At the subconscious level, I believe that being poor is more spiritual than being rich.

At the subconscious level, I believe it is possible for me to be wealthy at this time.

At the subconscious level, I believe that being rich will cause people to be jealous of me

At the subconscious level, I believe that being rich will keep me from entering heaven.

At the subconscious level, I feel that being poor is morally superior to being rich.

On a scale of 0 to 10, with 0 being no effect and 10 being the greatest positive effect, how effective would _____(insert method) be for clearing _____(name the block) quickly, easily, comfortably and with no negative side effects at this time?

For best results, how long would I need to apply/use _____(insert method) in order to permanently clear that block at that level?

For best results, how often would I need to apply/use_____(insert method) in order to permanently clear that block at that level?

On a scale of +10 to -10, with negative numbers being a bad outcome for my stated goals and priorities, what is the overall level in effects over the next _____(list a time period, like one year-as appropriate) of investing

On a scale of +10 to -10, what is the level of honesty and integrity in _____(the company or person) about this business venture/opportunity for me?

On a scale of 0 to 10, with 0 being not in alignment at all and 10 being optimally aligned, how aligned am I overall at this time on all levels of my being with being financially secure?

On a scale of 0 to 10, with 0 being not in alignment at all and 10 being optimally aligned, how aligned am I overall at this time on all levels of my being with being financially wealthy?

On a scale of 0 to 10, with 0 being not in alignment at all and 10 being optimally aligned, how aligned am I overall at this time on all levels of my being with quickly resolving my current financial challenges easily?

On a scale of 0 to 10, with 0 being no resonant energy and 10 being the most I can have, how much am I resonating with shame energy on all levels of my being at this time?

On a scale of 0 to 10, with 0 being no resonant energy and 10 being the most I can have, how much am I resonating with self-punishment energy on all levels of my being at this time?

On a scale of 0 to 10, with 0 being none and 10 being the most resonant energy I can have, how much am I resonating with powerlessness on all levels of my being at this time?

On a scale of 0 to 10, with 0 being none and 10 being the most resonant energy I can have, how much am I resonating with victimhood on all levels of my being at this time?

On a scale of +10 to -10, with positive numbers indicating a positive outcome based on all the goals I have listed, what is the ranking at this time of getting a _____(type of loan) from _____(source of loan)

On a scale of +10 to -10, with positive numbers meaning a positive outcome based on my goals, what is the value to me at this time of entering _____(name of debt consolidation program) and participating exactly as directed by them for as long as directed by them.

On a scale of +10 to -10, with positive numbers indicating a positive outcome for my listed goals, what is the value to me at this time of participating in _____(name of program).

On a scale of +10 to -10, with positive numbers indicating a positive outcome for my goals, what is the value to me at this time of declaring _____(type of bankruptcy).

On a scale of 0 to 10, with 0 being none and 10 being the most I could have, how much shame energy do I have at this time about my financial situation?

On a scale of 0 to 10, with 0 being none, how much self-punishment energy do I currently have active in my system due to my financial situation?

Do I believe on any level of my being that I deserve to be punished for my financial problems?

Do I believe on any level of my being that I am powerless to resolve my financial issues

Do I believe on any level of my being that I must resolve my financial issues on my own, without outside help?

Do I believe it is wrong for my debt to be forgiven, and that I must pay every bit back?

∽

Dowsing Deeper

THE QUESTIONS in this book have helped us transform our lives; save lots of money; become healthier and more successful. But can you improve on them? Of course you can!

Each person is an individual. You have your own point of view made up of your values, beliefs and how you define and rate things in terms of your preferences.

Your dowsing question will be affected by all these things. A question asked using Maggie Percy's definitions of terms and her goals will be a good question for her, but it may or may not be a perfect question for you.

The best way to be sure to get dowsing answers that work for you is to create your own questions. This section will guide you in how to do that. It's only for serious dowsers who really want to improve their accuracy, because they intend to use dowsing to make their life better, or to help others.

We believe that learning to ask good dowsing questions not only improves your dowsing; it makes you think about your beliefs, values and preferences, and that causes you to live more consciously, to question things and to actively choose to create the life you want.

. . .

What Are Your Goals?

Not everyone has the exact same goals. Some people don't even really HAVE goals. So the first thing to do is to know your goals and to think about them in detail, so that when you create a dowsing question, you have a clear purpose for asking it, and you are aiming to achieve your goals.

Good goals are detailed and personal. Not everyone has the same goals about money. Most people are out of balance with the energy of money. If you are out of balance, you won't be able to achieve your goals. Dowsing is a great way to test how balanced your money energy is.

If you are just in survival mode, your money energy is not balanced. Abundance is the birthright of all of us. If you are not experiencing abundance, you have blocks or imbalances you need to deal with. And it may take some time, because often those patterns are family patterns that you learned as a child, or even inherited genetically.

What would you like to experience in terms of money and finances? Don't limit yourself. While change probably won't come overnight, it likely won't come at all if you don't have goals. Aim high, but be prepared to work. Don't limit yourself just to having enough to get by, unless that is really what you want. Don't adopt other peoples' money values without being sure they are what you want.

List the things that you consider important factors in your dowsing answer. When you are making a dowsing question, the most important thing to start with is to know what goals you wish to achieve. Be very clear. If you have multiple goals, list them all.

Sometimes you need to do more than one question on a given situation. If the goals don't all directly relate to one subject, break them down.

. . .

WHAT DO YOUR WORDS MEAN?

Too often, you use words that you haven't clearly defined. You may
think you know what they mean, but you don't. If you use vague,
undefined terms, your answer won't necessarily be accurate for you.

We spoke earlier of not using vague terms like "good", "healthy",
"highest and greatest good". These words and phrase have vague
meanings, or none at all. Don't use them.

Instead, think about words that mean something specific to you and
relate to your goals. Some financial terms you could use would be "to
discharge all of my debt, either through the debt being forgiven or
some other means"; "to align myself and my energy with accepting all
the abundance the Universe is sending me"; "to balance myself with
healthy energies around the concept of money"; "to enhance my ability
to receive and be totally in the flow of abundance".

People use poor words when they are lazy, or if they lack confidence or
just are living unconsciously. Dowsing will help you question your
values and get you to act more consciously, which will help you
manifest positive outcomes.

Don't use other people's definitions of terms unless you are sure you
agree with them.

INCLUDE ALL The Parts Of A Good Question

Poor questions often are poor because they lack an important element.
A good question should include how, what, where, when, who
and why.

Time is a critical aspect that is often overlooked. "At this time" is a
good phrase to add to any question when you are testing about
something for right now.

Indicate whom you are dowsing about.

Include a specific time frame: "at this time"; "this program I am applying for now"; "within the next 90 days".

Name the specific program or support system you are considering. Drill down to make sure you locate a specific person or program that will give you the results you desire.

Be sure to include why you are asking the question; what is the goal.

A good dowsing question is usually long and detailed.

CHECK Your Answers

As often as possible, write down your question and your answer, and then after an appropriate time, check your answer for accuracy.

Sometimes the answer is accurate, but you left out an important part, so it appears to be wrong. Here's an example: Maggie dowsed that she would be given approval for a home loan modification. She had gone through a laborious process with Bank of America, and it dowsed that a home loan modification would be approved.

But she left something out. She left out 'when'. Because she was caught up in the filing of paperwork and was very focused on the present process, it didn't occur to her to add a time.

BAC rejected the application after 18 months of haggling. Maggie couldn't believe her dowsing, which had felt so accurate, was wrong, but she had to accept facts.

Then, 3 years later, the mortgage was sold to another company, who approached Maggie about applying for a home loan modification. Not being keen on going through 18 months of trouble, she was hesitant, but did it anyway. Within 3 months, approval came through, and the modification was granted.

Maggie's dowsing was right, but she only found that out later. Look at your question. If it appears wrong, ask yourself if you included ALL the aspects of a good question. Ask yourself how you could change the question and have it be correct. If Maggie had done that exercise, she might have realized that maybe the answer WAS correct, but not for that case.

Making mistakes is a great way to improve your dowsing if you take the time to check your answers and find ways to improve how you ask questions. Don't be upset if you make a mistake...learn from it!

STUDY Your Subject

Do not use dowsing as a substitute for educating yourself about money. Study up on the subject you are dowsing about. While you don't need to be an expert, having familiarity with financial terms and situations will help you create a better dowsing question.

Too often, we see money issues coming up because the person has avoided becoming familiar with finances; because the person avoids the whole concept of being responsible for her money situation; because the person feels incompetent with money, and so ignores finances as much as possible.

If you find yourself not being interested in your finances or avoiding doing things relating to accounting or budgeting, you are probably out of balance with healthy money energy. Examples include things like bouncing checks; making mistakes in your check register; hating balancing your checkbook; not having any budget; not wanting to discuss money and finance with your family members; not paying attention during the checkout process to the total of your shopping purchases; having your debit or credit cards hacked; losing your credit or debit cards.

Use dowsing to evaluate how balanced you are and to find a method that will help you align with abundance.

8

MISCELLANEOUS QUESTIONS

Moving To A New Location

MOVING CAN BE VERY traumatic for you, your family and pets. It's especially challenging if you aren't really certain you are going to the 'right' place. You put a lot of effort into relocating, but will it actually be what you wanted? You feel like you are gambling with your happiness. But dowsing will help you know how to make the 'right' move.

On important questions like moving, it is always best to have another dowser double check your answers or blind dowse to see if they agree with your answers.

Is It Time For A Move?

You may know you don't want to live here anymore. You may be aware that at some point, you will be moving to a new location. But timing is everything. Even if you go to the 'right' place, if it's the wrong time, things may go badly.

These questions are not to be used for predicting the future, because that is iffy at best. But you can evaluate the appropriateness of making a move now or in the very near future using these dowsing questions.

It's important to consider what goals you have for moving. Maybe taking a job in a new location will enhance your finances, but perhaps the pollution there will harm your health. Or maybe your children will do very badly in school there. Or your spouse may grow away from you, because he is not enjoying benefits from the move.

Please list all your goals before you dowse. Include health, finances, relationships, happiness, career, etc. Then get an overall score using the questions below.

You can also dowse the question for individual goals. For example, if you get a -2 overall for moving, maybe some aspect is -7, while others are +9. You can find out by dowsing the individual goals. Then you can decide if you are willing to compromise on any of them. Personally +8 or higher is what I'd aim for as an overall score.

On a scale of +10 to -10, with 0 being neutral and positive numbers being positive overall for my goals, what is the score for moving to _____*at this time/*_____*(or fill in a time)?*

WHERE TO GO AND WHY?

You may not have a choice of where to move. But then, maybe you do. Maybe you are retiring and have a few locations you are considering. Or perhaps your job has a few other locations, and you could ask to relocate to any one of them. If you have a choice of where to move, then you can dowse and find out which place(s) are best for your goals.

To get accurate and useful answers, you need to have very clear goals. List what your goals for health, finances, relationship, career, happiness, hobbies, etc are. Then you can dowse an overall rating or get a score for each goal.

If you know the places you want to test, you can use this question, putting the location in the blank:

On a scale of +10 to -10, with 0 being neutral and positive numbers being positive overall for my goals, what is the score for moving to _____at this time/_____(or fill in a time)?

If you don't really have particular places in mind, that can be tricky to dowse. It's better to have some overall idea of your preference as to climate, lifestyle choices, etc, and then have some locations you think are worth testing.

Map Dowsing:

As a last resort, as long as you are very clear about your goals, you can map dowse for general locations. In the US, for example, you could dowse over a US map to ask which states have locations that would be an 8 or higher overall for your goals. Point at each state and ask:

On a scale of +10 to -10 for my goals overall, is there any location in this state that is +8 or better for me to move to at this time?

The same principle can be used on a map of any country, testing provinces, counties or other large areas. You can then get a list of towns or cities in the area that tests best and test each town or city.

List Dowsing:

List dowsing is another form of dowsing like map dowsing. Instead of a map, you get a list of states, provinces, cities, countries, etc. Then you use the same question to find good prospects. If you are a very visual person, using a map might work better. Try both and see which feels best to you.

Of course, it makes sense to do your due diligence and study up on what that location is like. Get online. Read local papers. Find out about the economy, weather, crime and lifestyles to make sure it suits your needs.

~

Subconscious Beliefs

THE ROLE Of The Subconscious

For years we have used dowsing with our clients and ourselves to identify and remove blocks to personal growth. It is now becoming popular to talk about the role of the subconscious in blocks, so you have probably heard about it.

Your subconscious is tasked with keeping you safe. But it is loaded with a lot of faulty beliefs. Those beliefs are often in conflict with your conscious goals and beliefs. When this occurs, the subconscious wins, as it is in control most of the time.

If you aren't clear about the role of the subconscious, this might seem counter-intuitive. You know what you want. But that is your conscious mind. Your subconscious runs the show most of the time, and you cannot know what it wants. The term 'subconscious' means that it exists below the level of your conscious mind and out of its view.

In order to more easily achieve your conscious goals, you can discover and transform subconscious beliefs that are blocking you. Dowsing is probably the easiest way to do this. Dowsing gives you a direct line to what's going on at the subconscious level.

By asking simple questions, you can discover what your subconscious believes and then use dowsing to determine how to clear those beliefs.

DOWSING Subconscious Beliefs

There are an infinite number of beliefs you have at the subconscious level that are holding you back, but the biggest ones are about safety issues.

Your subconscious has beliefs that are related to perceived dangers to you: physical, emotional and spiritual. Any type of death: the death of your body, the loss of a dear loved one, the loss of your soul, will be avoided at all costs.

Unfortunately, you don't know what safety issues your subconscious has. Many of them have to do with things you are trying to achieve: health, happiness, wealth, success.

Another line of beliefs has to do with where your subconscious stands on taking action. Does it want to? Does it feel you are capable? Is it committed? Is it committed to doing it now?

These basic questions can be adapted to test any goal you have, at the subconscious level. The more blocks you have, the harder it will be to achieve your goal.

Create a phrase that summarizes your goal. Examples are: "lose 10 pounds in the next month", "win $1 million in the lottery", "be loved for myself", "get a promotion to manager this year", "become a bestselling author within 9 months".

Fill the blank with your goal and dowse the following:

I believe on all levels that it is safe for me to

_____.

On all levels, I want to _____.

On all levels, I believe I am able to _____.

On all levels, I have chosen to _____.

I have chosen to _____*now.*

These questions can be used to test any goal you have. By clearing those which are counter to your conscious desires, you clear the most fundamental blocks you have to success.

Another angle you can check is the 'shoulds' in your subconscious. It is common for the subconscious to have rigid rules to follow. Those may best be seen in statements that begin with "I must" or "I must not". This sense of rigid obligation is difficult, if not impossible, to overcome with conscious desire.

Think about the goal you have. Make a short phrase that summarizes your goal, such as, "being a successful entrepreneur" or "having a happy marriage with _____(your partner)". Now test it in this statement:

At the subconscious level, I believe I must not_____(put your goal in here).

Think about the negative pattern you are experiencing that is frustrating the heck out of you, such as, "I can't accumulate more than $100 in my savings account" or "I can't lose more than 10 pounds". Make a phrase the summarizes this pattern, such as, "never save more than $100", "never lose more than 10 pounds". Dowse this statement:

At the subconscious level, I believe I must _____(put the pattern here, such as 'never save more than $100).

More often than not, you will find that your subconscious believes you must not achieve your conscious goals, and it is restricting you to whatever the 'glass ceiling' is that you have been experiencing. Clearing these subconscious beliefs paves the way for future progress.

CLEARING Subconscious Beliefs

Once you identify your subconscious negative beliefs, you can clear them. Transform the energy of the beliefs using whatever method tests best. Any method can work. Some examples are symbols, colors, statements of intention, prayer, tapping, Emotion Code, Healing Codes, Spiritual Response Therapy.

It's best to have a variety of tools in your toolkit, as different beliefs have different frequencies, and there is no one method that will clear every faulty belief. Find some that work for you. Start with simple ones that cost little, like color or symbol therapy or statements of intention.

Once you have used the method you chose, go back and retest the belief. On rare occasions, it may take a day or two for the energy to transform, so you might want to test whether the statement will be true in 3 days.

If you find the belief did not clear, try another method. If that does not work, more than likely there is a belief that is propping the other one up, a bigger, stronger, deeper belief that you need to discover and clear so that the one you already found may be cleared.

When this happens, it takes a little special detective work to figure out what the issue is. I find that tuning in to the belief that won't shift and letting myself empty my mind and allow the answer to come to me works best. Just get in a meditative state and focus on asking what would be a likely belief or issue that would cause you to believe the belief that won't clear.

Here's one example: You have tried to clear a belief that says you must not accumulate more than $100 in savings. No matter how much you clear, that belief re-activates and you can't seem to accumulate funds.

Detach from any emotion and tune in to that belief. Acknowledge it and be ok about it. Your subconscious is just trying to protect you from harm. Quietly ask yourself why your subconscious keeps reactivating this belief; what is it afraid of? The first thing you think of is probably the belief you need to clear. If you think of more than one, clear them all. Here are some examples of things that might come to you:

If I am wealthy, my family will reject me.

If I accumulate money, I will be robbed or cheated.

If I accumulate savings, I will be killed.

Something will come to you. You will think you made it up. Test it anyway. Clear it. Then clear the original belief and retest it. Usually this works well. But you will have to be patient and trusting to develop the ability to do this easily. It takes time and effort. Just do it.

Remember, the beliefs behind the one you tried to clear are probably very powerful, related to your safety or that of your loved ones and usually don't make a lot of sense in the context of this life and your conscious goals.

Please note: many of the subconscious beliefs you will uncover sound really, really stupid to your conscious mind. Everyone has silly subconscious beliefs that do not make logical sense at all. Being open to finding that you have beliefs like this is important. Don't judge. Just laugh about them and clear them.

IT'S NEVER-ENDING...

If you get into the mindset that clearing all your faulty beliefs is the best or only way to achieve your goals...don't. It's a temptation we got sucked into early on, and it took us years to realize that it is an endless process.

You will always have faulty beliefs or other mechanisms blocking you, but you don't have to clear all of them to succeed. Certainly, clearing key issues can be helpful in speeding your progress. But focusing only on what's wrong is backwards. And it tends to lock you into a negative circle. You end up feeling you will never be deserving of success.

. . .

A Better Way…Create What You Want

While there's no harm in identifying and clearing blocks, don't let that be your only or even your main focus. Spend an equal or greater amount of time deciding what it is you DO want.

Be specific. Make a detailed list. Then spend time creating an action plan. Then take action.

We have studied the Law of Attraction for some years, and it really appeals to us. By focusing on what is good in our lives, we have attracted more of the same. By being grateful for what we have, we have attracted more.

It is not a simple or straight line to your goal, but just keep making course corrections. Release or clear energies that don't resonate with your goals. Learn to love and accept yourself as you are. Judging or rejecting yourself is one of the biggest blocks to success, perhaps THE biggest one. Acknowledge that this is a journey of transformation. Choose to enjoy it. Invest the time and have fun. Don't dwell on what hasn't materialized for you yet.

Dowsing done properly can help you balance your heart and your head, the rational and the intuitive. Dowsing can help you learn to 'know' that even when it doesn't look good, things are unfolding in the best way for your long term happiness and goals.

Making Important Choices

Left Brain vs. Right Brain: Strengths and Weaknesses

You have probably heard about the differences between your left and right brain. The left brain is more rational and logical, while the right brain is more creative and intuitive.

Why do think you have two different brains? The answer is obvious.

Each has unique strengths, and using both sides appropriately gives the best results.

Unfortunately, in our society, the left brain is king, especially since Science became the new religion. One or two hundred years ago, no one would have said, "That must be wrong, because it hasn't been scientifically proven." Back then, nothing was scientifically proven in double blind studies in labs. Instead, people judged something based on their own experience or that of many others like them. This type of wisdom has been labeled 'old wives' tales', but in recent years, Science has come around to realizing much of that wisdom has truth.

Rigorous scientific methods have their uses, just like the left brain does. But not allowing the right brain to be an equal partner is the same as tying one arm behind your back. Would you purposely hinder yourself day in and day out by doing that? Of course not. Yet time and again, you hear people invoke Science (most of them not really knowing anything about it) as if Science is the final word on every topic.

The plain fact is that although modern science has given us many wonderful gifts, it is very far from having all the answers. In fact, Science is pretty lame at having answers to the really important things in life, things that most of us want: happiness, love, peace and success.

It seems the things we value most are of the heart. And in that, they are more right brain functions. They aren't logical, and you can't easily explain them, but we believe in them. (Or at least most of us do.) So why do people treat the right brain like Cinderella? Why do we find psychic or artistic or creative talent fascinating, yet put it down as not scientific, and thus worth-less?

As a dowser, you will find that making a good dowsing question is the strength of the left brain. It can pick words, analyze and create a detailed question. The right brain, however, is what you need for the actual dowsing of the question. At that point, the left brain needs to stand down.

Many of the problems people experience with dowsing have to do with their trying to dowse with only one side of the brain. That generally gives poor results.

Left brain dominant dowsers may excel at creating good dowsing questions, but they will be challenged to let go of control of the process when they actually dowse. The left brain seeks control and wants to always be right, and thus wants to predict the correct answer. If you are left brain dominant and you do not release control, you will tend to always get the answers you expect, and many times, they will be wrong.

Right brain dominant people tend to excel at the actual process of dowsing. They connect with their intuition easily, and they are willing to let go of control. But they are often weak at asking a good dowsing question. They want to get right to the part they love, and they skip the boring and tedious process of creating a logical, detailed question. They, too, will often get wrong answers to their dowsing.

It is beyond the scope of this book to try and explain the differences between left and right brain in detail, but it is important that you understand that dowsing properly requires both sides of the brain. In fact, it is a brain-balancing activity. So you will find that you need to force yourself to use your weaker or less preferred side of the brain if you want to become a good dowser. It takes practice, and in doing so, you will reap many unexpected benefits. You may have noticed the theme throughout this book that an investment of time and effort will be required to become a master dowser, but if you invest, you can succeed.

MAKING Big Decisions

Dowsing is valuable for making all kinds of decisions, but it's the big ones that really pay off. Marrying the wrong person; taking the wrong job; moving to the wrong location; these are things that cost you a lot of money, time, effort and heartache. Ultimately, the stress of making a bad decision can ruin your health!

Dowsing is valuable for simple daily choices, but nothing will give you a bigger high than using dowsing for big decisions that have a lot riding on them. Dowsing helped us realize we were meant to be together. It has helped us pick the perfect home to buy and guided us on major decisions in our business and health.

Do you always make the right choice if you dowse? No. But you make the right choice more often than if you aren't a dowser. **And that's the only way to measure its value.**

You're going to take a job, get married or move to a new location at some point in your life. But if you try to make that decision only using half your brain, you are handicapping yourself. Sometimes you'll pick right, but other times you won't. For most of our lives we didn't use dowsing. We didn't know about it. Once we discovered dowsing and started using it regularly, we had a much higher percentage of good choices than in the past.

One of the hardest things about using dowsing for big decisions is to trust the answer. Especially if the answer is unexpected. Start small and go with your dowsing answers. Use 'mistakes' to improve your technique. (Note: you can only tell if you made a mistake if you are dowsing something measurable, so be sure to do that often.) When you are ready, start using dowsing for bigger decisions. You will see that overall, your decisions get better and better.

TRICKS Of The Trade

We've covered a lot of specific dowsing topics in other chapters. Here, we will share some techniques that work for any big decision, tips that will help you get more accurate answers to those important questions.

Here are a few questions we discovered over the years that kept us from tripping up on big questions:

*If I _____(buy this/marry her/take this job/etc), how happy will
I be with my decision overall in _____(pick an appropriate time
frame, like 1 year/5 years).*

This question is designed to remove you from whatever emotion you
are currently feeling and tap into how this choice will affect you in the
long run. Important decisions are important largely because they have
such a huge long term impact on your health, finances or happiness.

Am I able to get an accurate answer to this question at this time?

Sometimes you want to dowse something that you aren't ready or able
to get a correct answer to. For some reason, you will tend to get an
accurate answer to this question. If you get that you cannot get an
accurate answer to the specific dowsing question you have, don't
dowse it.

Am I lying?

Ask your dowsing question, then using the definition of 'lying' to be
that some part of you is supplying an incorrect answer, ask "Am I
lying?" This is not about conscious lying. It is about subconscious
lying. If you get that you are lying, then more than likely, the correct
answer to your original dowsing question is the opposite to what
you got.

Although this question might be surprising, it certainly does work,
even though we don't really have an explanation as to why it works. In
our opinion, if it works, use it. Explanations can come along later.

These simple questions have helped us avoid dowsing disaster
many times.

∾

Major Purchases

As Always, **Start With Your Goals**

If you read this book from the beginning, you are probably tired of hearing this. But it is one of the most important things you can learn to do if you want to be an accurate dowser. Just grabbing your pendulum and dowsing is a big mistake.

Focusing on your goals helps you to really get a good dowsing question. That leads to a better answer. But a side effect is that by learning to constantly focus on your goals, you will also become better at manifesting them.

Truth is, most people don't focus on what they want. They focus on 'what is', which is usually not what they want. Dowsing can help you become a much better manifester by helping you become clear on what you want.

When you are going to spend big money to buy a house, a car or to take an expensive vacation, dowsing can save you a ton of time, effort and money. So take the time to make a list of what exactly you want in a car/house/vacation. Be specific and let it cover all possible subjects.

THINK **About How Exactly You Measure Success**

Big purchases will have unique aspects you want to think about when you dowse. For most of them, you want the object to be in good condition and not in need of major repair now or any time in the near future. You want the item to be as described in the ad. You have an idea of why you might buy this item. And the why might be very personal for you.

Is it in how happy you are with it in a certain time frame?

Lack of repairs?

Cost effectiveness?

Or some specific goal you have that is unique to you?

Resale value?

Quality of workmanship?

How well it's backed up with support or a warranty?

Value for the price?

There are many possible things you can add to your list. Take your time and think about them. Then put a question together that speaks to your needs and goals.

Dowsing Questions

The following are sample questions about major purchases, but it would be best for you to refine them to suit your particular situation.

On a scale of +10 to -10, with negative numbers being a poor score, what does this car/job/location/whatever rank overall for my goals?

If I buy this _____(car/sound system/computer), how happy would I be 1 year (or name a time) after buying it on a scale of 0-10, with 10 being ecstatic.

On a scale of +10 to -10, with positive numbers being good, how does this product rank overall for value for the price?

On a scale of 0-10, with 10 being best, how good is the warranty/service on this product?

Generally we don't invest in things that test lower than an 8. You don't want to make a major purchase and find it doesn't live up to your expectations. Keep looking and researching until you find something that dowses as very good. Ideally, a 10 would be great, but sometimes there aren't any 10s available.

∼

Buying Gifts

What Do You Want The Gift To Do?

Are you sick of hearing it yet? You need to be very clear what your goals are for buying this gift, or you may not be satisfied with the results.

Are you just doing it because you have to show up with something? Well, then your gift won't wow the recipient.

Are you wanting the person to be amazed and fall in love with you or whatever you gave? That requires a bit of thought.

Are you on a budget? Do you want to shop online or in person? Do you only want to go to the mall and find something in one of the shops there? Write down what your specific desires are and build them into the question as your 'goals'.

Dowsing has helped us to choose gifts that are very well-received. Likewise, it has helped us avoid disappointing ones. I'm sure you've experienced that, where you spent a lot of time trying to find the perfect gift for a loved one. Then you gave it to her and found out she already had one; it was the wrong size; she wouldn't use it; she really didn't like it that much.

I think everyone has been disappointed in their gift giving, and this is an area that both newbies and veteran dowsers can put to the test right away and see great results.

The following sections address key aspects of dowsing for success in giving great gifts.

What To Give?

Dowsing probably is a bit harder to do on this topic. If you have no clue what the recipient likes, dowsing can help you, but I find it much better at narrowing down choices once you have a better idea of what you intend to get.

In spite of that, you can use dowsing to check out what category of gift would go over best. Some of the categories you can consider could be: clothing, candy or other consumable (gourmet food and wine), electronics, jewelry, hobby stuff, books, music, DVDs, small appliances, accessories of any kind, tickets to an event or movie, gift certificate of some type.

You can make a list of all the categories you would consider, then assign each a unique number. Then dowse which category has the best gift idea that you are able to buy online or locally for your price range.

Of the categories in this list, which category has the best gift for my goals?

Note this is like scale dowsing in that you don't get a simple yes/no answer. You can list dowse a list of all the numbers or even the names of the categories, running your finger down the list as your pendulum swings in a neutral swing, waiting for the 'yes' to show you the answer. Then double check the category you chose.

DOES SHE HAVE ONE?

It is so disappointing to buy a gift that is a duplicate of something your loved one already has. So you definitely want to check that she doesn't have one, once you determine what it is you intend to buy.

Does _____(name of recipient) already have _____(a copy of a particular book/tickets to a specific event/a jacket just like this) at this time?

WILL SHE LIKE IT?

Whether she has one or not, it's important to assure yourself that the investment you make is going to make her very happy. So check that out.

On a scale of +10 to -10, with negative numbers meaning she won't like it,

how will _____ *(recipient's name) like this item if I give it*
to her as a _____ *(name the occasion) gift?*

I sure wished my father had used this question and dowsed about gifts
he gave my mother. His gifts always made her angry. He would give
her appliances and work-saving devices like a new vacuum. To her,
that represented her enslavement to housework and seemed like a slap
for how she was doing it. He never figured it out, because they never
talked about anything.

WILL SHE USE IT?

We discovered this tricky little aspect one day when dowsing a gift for
Maggie's Dad. We found a jacket we thought would look sharp on him,
and we dowsed he'd like it. It was a leather jacket that was very nice.
But something told us to ask if he would use it, and the answer came
out 'no'. Don't be bummed out by having your gift sit on a shelf
forever.

If I give this item to _____ *(person's name) as a*
_____ *(occasion) gift, will he/she use it?*

WHERE Is The Best Place To Buy It?

You many have a preference for buying online. Or perhaps you want
to go to the mall. Maybe you don't want to drive too far.

Another thing that enters into where you buy a gift is price. Some
places have the same item for a lower price. Or maybe you get better
service or a good guarantee somewhere.

Be clear what your goals are with respect to the place you intend to
buy it, then dowse.

On a scale of +10 to -10, with negative numbers being bad, how does
_____ *(name of store) rate for buying*

_____(name the exact item) as a gift _____(name the time frame, like 'this week'--they may be out of stock)?

~

Past Lives

Past Lives Affect This One; But It Isn't Just Past

It is beyond the scope of this book to teach you everything about past lives, but since they can have such a big effect on your current life, and since dowsing is a powerful tool, we want to touch briefly on this subject and how dowsing can help you deal with past life issues.

The first thing you need to understand is that it isn't just past lives. It's future lives. Parallel lives. Some other type of lives. So you might to just want to refer to them all as 'other lifetimes', meaning not the current one.

No one can really prove or even explain well how the whole concept of time works. It's generally believed that time is not linear, though it appears that way to us. Many believe that all lives are being lived simultaneously, even though that seems strange.

How about parallel lives? They are in 'current' time, but not the same life as this one. I think of them as a continuum of lives. They exist next to each other in an infinite series. Each lifetime that is adjacent has more in common than those farther away in the continuum.

For parallel lives, think of each life as being a unique set of energy frequencies that creates the situation. Since you are able to shift energy, you can therefore shift into another reality. It would seem to be easier on the whole to shift to one closer to this one. Instead of suggesting you could wake up and find you have no children or a different husband (as in some movies), you just wake up and things seem a bit 'different'. Over time, if you are doing lots of transformational work, those differences pile up. At some point, you feel like a totally different person than you once were.

It's hard to picture all the different times and the many variations possible in each of them and think of them all existing simultaneously. It's mind-boggling. But thank heaven, you don't really need to understand the physics of it or be able to explain it in order to dowse about them.

THERE ARE Many Resources

We aren't teaching you clearing methods in this book. But there are a number of good ways to clear energies from other lifetimes. Here are a few that we have found useful:

Spiritual Response Therapy: SRT was created by Robert Detzler. We were both certified in the method while living in the U.K. We practiced it for ourselves and our clients for a number of years before moving on to other methods. SRT uses charts and dowsing to identify causes of problems and their 'cures'. It healed Maggie of a lifelong dairy allergy and Nigel of a lifelong cheese allergy. Past lives are a big aspect of this healing process.

Charts: You can buy or make charts and use them to dowse about other lifetimes in similar fashion to those used in SRT.

Experts: There are many dowsing professionals who offer sessions to help you discover and clear issues from other lifetimes. Research carefully before working with someone and make sure she is a good match for you. This is a good option if you are not a confident dowser yet.

Books: There are any number of books about past lives and other lifetimes and how they can affect you. It's great not to have to reinvent the wheel. Read up on the subject and see what makes sense to you.

· · ·

BASIC DOWSING ABOUT PAST LIVES/OTHER LIVES

If you want to find out more about another lifetime, there are some key questions you can dowse. If you have charts, like those used in Spiritual Response Therapy, they are an easy way to get information.

If you don't have charts, practice 'tuning in' to the energy of that lifetime as you dowse. You may be surprised how often you get impressions, see scenes or just 'know' about them. Much of the detail I get about other lives now comes from just doing this when dowsing, and letting the information come through in bigger chunks than just 'yes' or 'no'.

Be patient about developing the ability to do this, but if you are dowsing properly, not focusing only on your tool, but focusing on being open to receiving the information, you will get more and more detail. For some, this may take a lot of practice. I am convinced that with time and practice, you can increase your ability to access this information.

You can use the following questions to gather details of other lifetimes so that you can clear them or the issues. Sometimes you 'need' to know a certain amount about another lifetime before you can let go of that energy. You can use dowsing to determine if you need details, and how many details you need to get.

When was it?

This one is tough, because we apparently perceive time wrongly. But I usually go with the following: past life, parallel life, future life.

Is the lifetime I am researching a Past life? Future life? Parallel life?

Then if you want, you can pinpoint where on the timeline the life falls. So for a future life, you can ask:

Is this life more than 100 years in the future? (Change numbers to narrow it down).

If yes, then substitute larger and larger numbers until you get 'no'. If the original answer is 'no', then substitute smaller and smaller numbers until you get 'yes'.

Who/what were you?

Was I human? Male? Female?

You might be surprised to find other lifetimes where you were an animal or a gaseous being in space. Use your imagination if you were not human. Again, tuning in to the life often provides a quick answer that you can then test by dowsing.

Where was it?

Did this lifetime take place on earth? On another planet? In space?

What role did you have?

Was I a mother/priestess/political leader/religious leader/craftsman/healer/diviner?

Just keep naming roles until you get a 'yes'. Usually the other lives that are causing issues now have to do with a situation that could impact the present lifetime. So for example, if you find a past life affecting your ability to dowse, possibly you were using dowsing or intuition in that lifetime and were punished for it.

Death of yourself or a loved one is usually the thing that causes another life to be negatively affecting you. Your subconscious created a belief in that life that dowsing was bad and would kill you, and it activated in this lifetime when you learned dowsing.

What was this about?

Based on the issue you are working to resolve, you might have some hints as to what this is. Often there will be a similarity to this lifetime. So if your issue is about becoming powerful, then that lifetime may have had to do with the abuse of power. Or if your current issue is about money, that other lifetime probably had to do with wealth backfiring. If you are unsuccessful as a healer in this life, maybe you were burned at the stake in a past life for being a great healer.

It's hard to give you exact questions on this. Just follow where you are led. Some possible starting points are:

Was this about power? Wealth? Business? Politics? Religion? Love?

Who was involved?

There will be a cast of characters in the other lifetime. Usually it will have been someone close to you. Random violence and betrayal sometimes leaves a scar on your subconscious, especially if it's a huge movement that put you to death, but in general, more often, there are individuals who 'did you wrong'.

Were the major conflicts with an individual? A government? A religious organization? A political group?

Was it a family member? A blood relative? Someone related to me by marriage? A business partner? A lover?

Did you die? How?

Did I die physically as a result of the situation? Did someone close to me die as a result?

The death of you or a loved one is the most common cause of a faulty belief from another lifetime. Though physical death is the most common, there is also spiritual or emotional death, as in losing the love of someone who matters to you or feeling you have been condemned to hell. In some cases, the belief may have been caused by you going totally bankrupt and then not being able to support your family, who became ill or died.

CLEARING **the energy**

When you dowse that you have found out all you need to know in order to clear the energy, then perform the clearing. Usually you can just disconnect from that other lifetime and clear the belief or the energies that came over. Sometimes a simple prayer or statement of intention works; other times, you need to use something more complex. Dowsing will help you pick the best method. Then dowse and check results.

Connections To Past Lives

We've had clients who shared that they tapped into another lifetime so they could enhance their power, talent or some aspect of their present life. Thinking like that will form a connection to a life that has an experience like you are seeking, but the down side is you can't just tap into your success and talent in another life. When the connection is made, everything from that life can affect you. Both the bad and the good. It is never to your advantage to consciously connect to another life.

You have all the talent and resources you need to succeed in this life. We are never sent here unable to achieve our goals. You may have to work, but you have all the tools you need to succeed. So, trying to tap into another life because you feel you arrived here unprepared is a sign of victim and powerlessness energy that you might want to work on.

You can ask if you have any connections to other lives at this time:

Do I have any active energetic connections to other lifetimes at this time?

You can dowse how many you have, if you like. But you don't need to know that in order to clear the connections most of the time. You can use statements of intention:

1. Please disconnect me from any other lifetimes that I am currently energetically connected to.

2. Please clear all issues that perpetuated those connections.

3. Please clear any energies that came over as a result of those connections.

You can dowse to confirm the connections are no longer there and all issues are cleared.

All The Miscellaneous Questions

USE this chart to dowse whatever you like and watch progress over time. We include two blanks, so remember to save one for copying...

MOVING to a New Location

On a scale of +10 to -10, with 0 being neutral and positive numbers being positive overall for my goals, what is the score for moving to _____at this time / _____(or fill in a time)?

On a scale of +10 to -10, with 0 being neutral and positive numbers being positive overall for my goals, what is the score for moving to _____at this time / _____(or fill in a time)?

On a scale of +10 to -10 for my goals overall, is there any location in this state that is +8 or better for me to move to at this time?

Subconscious Beliefs

I believe on all levels that it is safe for me to _____.

On all levels, I want to _____.

On all levels, I believe I am able to _____.

On all levels, I have chosen to _____.

I have chosen to _____now.

At the subconscious level, I believe I must not_____(put your goal in here).

At the subconscious level, I believe I must _____(put the pattern here, such as 'never save more than $100).

Big Decisions

If I _____(buy this/marry her/take this job/etc), how happy will I be with my decision overall in _____(pick an appropriate time frame, like 1 year/5 years).

Am I able to get an accurate answer to this question at this time?

Am I lying?

Major Purchases

On a scale of +10 to -10, with negative numbers being a poor score, what does this car/job/location/whatever rank overall for my goals?

If I buy this _____(car/sound system/computer), how happy would I be 1 year (or name a time) after buying it on a scale of 0-10, with 10 being ecstatic.

On a scale of +10 to -10, with positive numbers being good, how does this product rank overall for value for the price?

On a scale of 0-10, with 10 being best, how good is the warranty/service on this product?

Buying Gifts

Of the categories in this list, which category has the best gift for my goals?

Does _____(name of recipient) already have _____(a copy of a particular book/tickets to a specific event/a jacket just like this) at this time?

On a scale of +10 to -10, with negative numbers meaning she won't like it, how will _____(recipient's name) like this item if I give it to her as a _____(name the occasion) gift?

If I give this item to _____(person's name) as a
_____(occasion) gift, will he/she use it?

On a scale of +10 to -10, with negative numbers being bad, how does
_____(name of store) rate for buying
_____(name the exact item) as a gift
_____(name the time frame, like 'this week'--they may be out
of stock)?

Past Lives

Is the lifetime I am researching a past life? Future life? Parallel life?

s this life more than 100 years in the future? (Change numbers to
narrow it down).

Was I human? Male? Female?

Did this lifetime take place on earth? On another planet? In space?

Was I a mother/priestess/political leader/religious
leader/craftsman/healer/diviner?

Was this about power? Wealth? Business? Politics? Religion? Love?

Were the major conflicts with an individual? A government? A
religious organization? A political group?

Was it a family member? A blood relative? Someone related to me by
marriage? A business partner? A lover?

Did I die physically as a result of the situation? Did someone close to
me die as a result?

Do I have any active energetic connections to other lifetimes at
this time?

Tips & Tricks

If I _____(buy this/marry her/take this job/etc), how
happy will I be with my decision overall in _____(pick an
appropriate time frame, like 1 year/5 years)?

Am I able to get an accurate answer to this question at this time?

Am I lying?

Is this the appropriate time to ask about _____(your subject)?

Is this the appropriate time to decide about _____(your subject)?

Is this the appropriate time to act on/do something on_____(your subject)?

9

TIPS, TRICKS & PITFALLS

Expert Advice

THERE ARE many other subjects we could have included in this book, but our goal was to give you enough practice that you can see the pattern in the making of a good dowsing question. Once you see that pattern, it becomes much easier to create good dowsing questions on any topic.

In other words, if you don't see the dowsing question you want to use here, you can generalize how you can create a good dowsing question by reading and practicing the material in this book. It's a case of give a man a fish or teach a man to fish...We believe you can learn to ask excellent dowsing questions on any subject by generalizing what is taught in this book.

Don't be afraid to step beyond your comfort zone and apply what you have learned in this book to dowse about subjects not covered here.

GENERAL PROCEDURE For Making A Good Dowsing Question

A good dowsing question will cover all of the following that apply: who, what, where, when, how and why. Sometimes it is challenging to figure out how to apply these to your question, so let's give some examples.

"Who" is the person you are dowsing for. It may be you or your pet squirrel.

"What" is more obvious. It's usually the subject you are seeking details on. For example, it might be the best apple in the pile or the movie you'd most enjoy watching.

"Where" will not always apply, but it is important at times. It can refer to a particular store, a location that has geopathic stress or a place where you will find a lost object.

"When" is vital and often overlooked. "At this time" is the most common phrase we use regarding dowsing about something. If I want a supplement, I have a time frame I am referring to. I might be dowsing the effect of taking the supplement for 30 or 90 days. Or I may be asking about how happy I'll be with my new car in 1 year. Or I may be asking how my liver is functioning at this time.

"How" is a bit more complex. How can relate to the dosage regimen for a supplement: twice a day for two months. It can describe the manner you are planning to drink a bottle of wine you are testing. You can include that you will be drinking it with a steak dinner and certain veggies; if you don't include the food, the test of the wine may be inaccurate.

"Why" is your goal. If you are trying to restore the health of your stomach, that is your why for dowsing a particular enzyme or dietary regimen. If you don't clearly state the "why", your answer may not be correct.

A proper dowsing question is usually long and detailed. Write your question down, along with the answer, using the charts at the end of each chapter. Go back over time and check your answers and see if you were correct. If not, look at ways to improve your question, your detachment or other aspects of your technique.

OVERCOMING PITFALLS

There are some common pitfalls in dowsing that you will want to avoid. It is beyond the scope of this book to go into a lot of detail on dowsing technique. But we hope that you will want to improve your technique and will check out our other books and courses and the offerings of us and other teachers so you can become the best dowser you can be. We are all continually learning and growing in this dowsing journey. It never ends.

POLARITY REVERSAL

Polarity reversal happens for a number of reasons. The result is that your dowsing answer reverses, and you don't even know it. This is probably the most common dowsing problem people have. The body has a natural polarity, like a magnet. When that is reversed, your dowsing answers are backwards. 'Yes' becomes 'no', and 'no' becomes 'yes'. This is disastrous for a dowser, especially a newbie, who then feels she cannot trust her answers, because they don't make sense.

Dehydration, poor mineralization, attachment to a particular answer, geopathic stress and strong emotions are the most common causes of polarity reversal. Make sure you are properly hydrated when dowsing. Keep your electrolytes balanced and make sure you have no mineral deficiencies. We have observed that dowsing and other intuitive activities like healing tend to 'burn' the frequencies of water, minerals and electrolytes, causing depletion. These lead to polarity reversal, so take care of your physical body.

Make sure you are dowsing in harmonious space away from noxious energies if possible. Noxious energies can flip your polarity.

Do not dowse when you are feeling strong emotions, especially fear. These cause you to become reversed. Practice detachment to help overcome this challenge.

Dowsing State Issues

Another very common pitfall is not being in a dowsing state. Many people are not taught how to get into a dowsing state. They don't even realize what it is or why it's important.

Dowsing answers do not come to you while you are in a normal attentive state. You need to be in what is called a 'dowsing state' to receive the answers. The dowsing state is an altered state that is a combination of detachment and emptying your mind while holding your focus only on the dowsing question and allowing the answer to come through. It is a peaceful and calm state that has no emotions or preconceived ideas.

Relaxation and meditation techniques can be helpful for getting into a dowsing state. You want to still the mind chatter. You want to release all emotions. You want to be fully receptive. You do not want to focus on anything except the dowsing question. This focus makes the dowsing state different from a meditative one, which has no focus at all.

Most people require practice to get into a dowsing state, but it becomes easier the more you do it. We recommend that you start dowsing in a quiet, safe and harmonious space away from anyone. As you gain confidence, you can begin to dowse in public, around other people and with distractions nearby. But don't try that at first.

We recommend you take our online dowsing course to learn all the basics and improve your dowsing accuracy. For details, visit The Dowsing Store online or visit this page for details of the course.

· · ·

Detachment

The left brain, the rational part of your mind, wants to be in control. But when dowsing, you cannot allow that. You need to tell the left brain to be the faithful servant. Sit down and shut up! The left brain helps you create the perfect dowsing question, but it cannot dowse. It needs to be quiet and let the right brain do that.

If you are someone with a strong mental energy, you may find this difficult. But if you skip learning to do this, you won't become a good dowser. Too many people use dowsing to rationalize the choices their left brain wants to make. They aren't interested in the truth or surprising answers that might cause them to question their current beliefs or prejudices.

Emotional detachment is vital to accurate dowsing. If you fear the answer or are attached to getting a particular answer, you probably won't get the right answer.

Don't try to dowse about life or death issues until you have done a lot of dowsing on everyday stuff to build your confidence. As you dowse about more things, you will gain confidence and find it easier to be detached. Being detached is like being curious. "I wonder" what the answer is. Be open to being surprised. Getting a surprising answer is often a sign of accurate dowsing.

One way to enhance detachment is to say "I wonder_____" many times a day, filling in the blank and letting whatever answer comes to mind appear and then let it go. Practice accepting whatever the answer is without judgment and release emotion. Judgment and emotion won't change reality; they just make it harder to take.

Helpful Tricks: Blind Dowsing And Dowsing Buddies

To help when dowsing about things that are important, you can fall back on blind dowsing or a dowsing buddy. Blind dowsing is simply hiding the answers so you don't know which one you are picking.

Blind dowsing is so helpful, we have an expanded version in the Appendices.

We like to write 'yes' and 'no' on several different pieces of identical paper, scrunch each one up and throw them on the floor. The ask your dowsing question and point your finger at one of the scrunched papers and ask, "Is this the correct answer to that question?" When you get a 'yes', open the paper and read the answer.

Having several papers helps avoid you guessing which are 'yes' and which are 'no'. If your answers are several different options, they can be written on scraps of paper and dowsed in the same way. We did this with a friend who couldn't decide which two kittens to adopt from the litter we fostered. She was thrilled with the results.

If you are attached to a certain answer, you will be tempted to re-dowse. Don't. Never re-dowse unless you change the question significantly. If you want to re-dowse, that is a sure sign that you are attached to a particular answer.

Having a dowsing buddy is another great way to help when you have emotional attachment to a certain answer. Make friends with someone who dowses and thinks the way you do about things. Ask that person to dowse your question and give you the answer. You can write the question down and just ask her to dowse whether the answer is 'yes' or 'no' to that question. You don't have to tell her the exact question.

If you have more than one question, you can write them down and number them and ask your dowsing buddy to give you the answers (yes or no) to questions that you have numbered 1 through 5.

Another way you can do this is ask your dowsing buddy how accurate your dowsing answer was to a certain question. Again, you do not have to tell her the question. Just ask on a scale of 0-10 with 10 being most accurate, how accurate was your dowsing. If it isn't at least 8, then you need to do some more dowsing.

. . .

TRICKS **Of The Trade**

We've covered a lot of specific dowsing topics in other chapters. Here, we will share some techniques that work for any big decision, tips that will help you get more accurate answers to those important questions.

Here are a few questions we discovered over the years that kept us from tripping up on big questions:

If I _____(buy this/marry her/take this job/etc), how happy will I be with my decision overall in _____(pick an appropriate time frame, like 1 year/5 years)?

This question is designed to remove you from whatever emotion you are currently feeling and tap into how this choice will affect you in the long run. Important decisions are important largely because they have such a huge long term impact on your health, finances or happiness.

Am I able to get an accurate answer to this question at this time?

Sometimes you want to dowse something that you aren't ready or able to get a correct answer to. For some reason, you will tend to get an accurate answer to this question. If you get that you cannot get an accurate answer to the specific dowsing question you have, don't dowse it.

Am I lying?

Ask your dowsing question, then using the definition of 'lying' to be that some part of you is supplying an incorrect answer, ask "Am I lying?" This is not about conscious lying. It is about subconscious lying. If you get that you are lying, then more than likely, the correct answer is the opposite to what you got.

These simple questions have helped us avoid dowsing disaster many times.

ASK, **Decide Or Do: A Great Way To Avoid Mistakes**

Nigel has a set of three questions which have been very helpful to us. Often, we are tempted to dowse about something at an inappropriate time. If you do that, the answers are useless.

So Nigel asks:

Is this the appropriate time to ask about _____*(your subject)?*

Is this the appropriate time to decide about _____*(your subject)?*

*Is this the appropriate time to act on/do something on*_____*(your subject)?*

In many cases, you will find that you do NOT get 'yes' to all of them. Only do whatever your dowsing indicates is appropriate at this time. Timing is vital, and this will help you avoid mistakes that might not be rationally obvious. Too often, we can get carried away with a great idea whose time has not yet come.

Note: These questions are listed in the "All the Questions" section of the Miscellaneous Questions chapter.

APPENDICES

List Dowsing

AT ONE POINT OR ANOTHER, every dowser will need to be able to dowse a list to find a specific answer to the question.

The list could be short or very, very long (as in a dictionary!)

Some of the possible reasons to dowse a list could include such problems as

- Selecting the best medical professional for your needs
- Choosing which therapy to use
- Choosing an item from a menu
- Selecting a homeopathic remedy or an essential oil
- Selecting a purchase from a catalog
- Selecting a word or words to help identify issues for your self-work
- Identifying a color to use
- Choosing from a list of numbers to find which one applies in your situation (e.g. Frequencies)
- And so on...

In other words, you can see that list dowsing has a wide range of possible uses. The step necessary for successful list dowsing will vary only slightly, based on whether you are working with very long lists or much shorter ones.

THE BASICS

No matter what your purpose for using a list, and no matter what size the list is or what form it is in (Yellow Pages, book, printed catalog or menu etc),

- always be in the dowsing state before you begin and
- always ensure that you have a precise and meaningful question in mind.

The question must be able to be answered by one or more items on the list (assuming you have already asked if the list holds the answer you are after!).

How that answer is indicated will depend on how you choose to dowse. A pendulum or other tool will be expected to respond positively to the correct answer or answers. If you are not using a tool, then you must be able to identify your personal positive and negative responses.

FOR SHORT LISTS

This is the simplest version and will work well with a list of up to about 20 items.

With the question in mind, point at each time in turn and await the response. It is possible to reduce the amount of time by only asking that a positive response is given and that you don't bother with negatives. Some dowsers are happiest with having the tool showing a 'ready' or negative response and then having it change to positive when the correct item or items are pointed at.

Depending on the speed of your dowsing reaction, you can choose whichever will give you the most secure response.

Be aware that you might well get the start of a positive response on the item prior to the actual one. So, you might need to check which of the two possible ones it is (assuming that only one item is the correct answer).

For Longer Lists

For any set of items which would take too long or be too tiring to dowse individually, the following process works very well indeed.

First, divide up the whole list into two halves. With a book, you can do this physically by holding half of the pages in each hand. With smaller, less easy to handle lists, you can mentally divide it into sections as outlined below:

For lists with several columns

- Ask which column it is in.
- Once the column is identified, then ask whether it is in the top or the bottom half of the column. If that reduces the number of possible items to about twenty or less, proceed as if it is now a Short List (above).

For lists with several pages up to the hundreds or even thousands. (This also works well with packs of cards).

- Divide them into two sections and ask which section the answer is in.
- Take that section and divide it again into two and repeat the question.
- Repeat this division until you are left with just a few pages.

- You can now dowse which page it is on
- Once the correct page is found, then you can isolate the item as before by column or by top and bottom until a reasonably small list is left to dowse one at a time.

The important thing to remember in this is that whenever you are faced with what looks like a large number of possible answers, simply create a list yourself from them (they may already be in a list), use the techniques above to reduce the numbers as quickly and efficiently as possible.

You might hear some dowsers referring to this technique as 'chunking down'.

Blind Dowsing

BLIND DOWSING, despite the term, does not mean that you blindfold yourself. Instead it refers to hiding the answers from yourself.

This is a particularly useful technique when you are dowsing about something to which you are emotionally attached, and you cannot find anyone else who is detached to dowse for you.

YOU MUST BE In A Dowsing State!

As with every other dowsing technique, you must be in the dowsing state and be able to have positive and negative responses before you begin.

To explain this clearly, let us use the following example.

Imagine that you are dowsing about the likelihood of a particular subject area coming up in an important test you have to pass. The answer is either yes or no, but it's something you have strong feelings about and so you feel you can't be objective it. The answer is to blind dowse the answer.

To do this you will need several pieces of identical paper. Cutting up a sheet of paper into about six or eight pieces will work well. Having an even number is important.

Write the word YES on half of the pieces and NO on the other half and then fold or crumple them up. This part is very important. The words must not be visible and there must not be an obvious way of noting which answer is which. So, for example, avoid pressing too hard or writing in thick black ink, having one piece of paper a much smaller or bigger size than the rest. You are trying to have all the pieces look as similar as possible.

Once you have achieved this, the next step is to shake them up, mix them around (in your hand or a container such as a box or bag) and then toss them on to a surface such as the table top or the floor, which ever is more convenient. Don't let them be spread too far apart.

Now, have you question clearly in mind and take your dowsing tool and dowse over the papers until you get a response.

THIS NEXT POINT IS ABSOLUTELY CRITICAL!.....

Take the paper, open it and ACCEPT THE ANSWER. That means, do not re-dowse or re-shuffle or anything else. The answer you got is the answer. It might not be the one you want, but that is the answer you get.

You can probably think of many other examples where you might feel too close to the subject to be able to dowse about it. Areas such as health, relationships and finances are obvious examples.

Having a dowsing buddy is always a great idea, but, for those times when it just isn't possible for one reason or another, this blind dowsing technique is invaluable.

But do remember, that the first answer you get is the answer. If you want to re-dowse because you want to 'check it again', that's a very good illustration of how emotionally involved you are with it all and how much you don't want to let go of controlling the situation!

Good luck!

Scales & How To Use Them

ONCE YOU HAVE MASTERED the dowsing response to get reliable positive and negative answers, you can then extend this principle to the use of scales.

Scales are remarkably flexible and can be used in a large number of ways.

Examples

For example, using scales you can

- estimate percentages

- work out the strength or weakness of an answer

- get a reading (from 1 to 10, for example) on how effective a solution or answer might be

- Finding the depth (or height) of an object

A scale can consist of anything; from the numbers 1 to 100, -10 to +10, to a range such as 'Poor, Below average, Average, Above average, Excellent'. You can probably think of some other examples yourself, depending on your circumstance.

When new dowsers are introduced to the dowsing state and then to the positive and negative responses, it can seem strange to then consider getting finer details to those answers. After all, a 'yes' is a 'yes' and a 'no' is a 'no', isn't it?

In fact, that is absolutely correct. In using scales, of any kind at all, the dowser is still looking to get a 'yes' or a 'no' response to the tool.

A Detailed Example

Let us look at how this works with an example for illustration.

Suppose you are dowsing about how effective a particular therapy or treatment would be for dealing with a physical issue facing you. There are various options (which you have discovered through the use of list dowsing) and you are left with deciding between three possible ones. Let's say that you are left with the following; reiki, re-bounding, and essential oils as the three solution which have dowsed as being beneficial.

But the real question now remains to be answered.... How beneficial will each of these be? Does it mean that you need all three?

Firstly, your dowsing indicates that only one of these will be necessary, although all of them are good for your issue. You do not need to combine any of them. You now need to decide which is the best for you, and by how much is it better for you?

This is where the use of scales is of great benefit.

Using Scales To Refine An Answer

Let's say that you will be using a scale of 0 to 10, with 10 being the most beneficial for resolving your physical issue quickly, safely, effectively and permanently. (NOTE: whenever you use a numeric scale, you MUST be quite clear in your mind what the extremes of the scale will represent for you.)

Using that as a guide, you dowse each of the three therapies and discover that reiki dowses as 7 out 10, re-bounding as 9 out of 10 and essential oils also dowses as 9 out of 10.

Now you have some useful information. You're going to discount reiki but you are left with two choices. At this point, you can decide, based on availability, cost and so on, which of the two you will pursue; oils or re-bounding. You will need to do some further dowsing to help you make that decision. For example, you might find that you only need one essential oil applied twice a day for three days as opposed to using a re-bounder once a day for three weeks. That's your choice. But the point is you will have discovered the two best approaches and you are in a better position to move forward.

It is not often that you are left with two identical results when using a scale. The above example will help you when you <u>are</u> faced with this situation.

Further Examples **Of Scales In Dowsing**

However, scales can be used to test when food is cooked to your liking, or how much you would prefer one bottled water over another. The possibilities, once you get used to the idea, are endless.

Other Examples

• How much more effective will one type of fertilizer be compared with another for your specific gardening needs?

• The advisability of going to a vet with an issue your pet has. Can you work to help the resolve the issue just as well or better, using tools you have?

• Which particular item from a menu in a restaurant new to you will you find the most enjoyable (because lots of them look great!)?

• How useful or welcome will your gift be for the intended recipient?

In other words, scales will help you to determine the best answer for you if there is more than one alternative. Scales will also be highly useful in determining the level of completion of various tasks, which can be useful in your self-work. Scales will also allow you to gain a better understanding of how useful, helpful or beneficial something is.

You may get free chart templates and scales at http://discoveringdowsing.com/scales-and-charts/

WHEN Not To Use Scales

Having said that, there are some occasions when scales are not useful. For example, if you decide to dowse something like the frequency or vibration of a food and then bless it and dowse it again afterwards to see how it has improved, that is a waste of the use of scales. After all, if you do not trust your own ability to bless anything or alter it with your intent, then it really doesn't matter about using dowsing. You will only be dowsing what you wish it to be, because there is no way you can objectively test it.

Similarly, it is a waste of time to dowse about the 'truth' of something. Unless you fully know which aspects are true and which are false and can understand the relative differences between them, all you are really doing is using your prejudices in your dowsing. (After all, you wouldn't dowse something as true or not if you didn't have a prejudice to begin with!)

Dowsing with scales to test the morality of a circumstance or to 'test' some unmeasurable aspect of a situation (such as frequency or a vibration, or the level of intent), is another way of renouncing your own rational ability, of going your power away. You can chose to believe whatever you want, but such situations can not be proven. Using scales, indeed, using dowsing at such times, is just a way of having your prejudices and opinions be shown to you via a dowsing response.

USE SCALES When It Makes Sense!

Keep the use of scales in dowsing to those areas which can be proven to yourself. Do not bother with trying to prove to anyone else the validity of your results. If you do this, the results will bear out the truth or otherwise of your dowsing. If nothing else, such results will help to improve your dowsing and help to make it a vital part of your life and not just an expression of your own opinions.

PLEASE LEAVE A REVIEW

Being able to ask a good dowsing question is one of the keys to success in dowsing. Please help us teach others how to dowse well by leaving an honest review wherever you bought this book.

RESOURCES

Books

Visit Sixth Sense Books at www.sixthsensebooks.com to see Maggie & Nigel's books about dowsing and related topics.

The Best Dowsing Course

Learn to dowse the right way in our DVD course. It includes basic and advanced training as well as tons of bonus material. Available in thumb drive or DVD set. See details here.
http://discoveringdowsing.com/dowsing-course

Free Dowsing Content

The Discovering Dowsing website at <u>http://discoveringdowsing.com</u> has free videos, a blog and articles on dowsing.

Free Scales & Chart Templates

You may get free chart templates and scales at <u>http://discoveringdowsing.com/scales-and-charts</u>

ABOUT THE AUTHORS

Maggie and Nigel met on a dowsing email group in 2000, and Maggie dowsed Nigel was meant to be her life partner, so she went to the UK to meet him. They married in the UK and returned to the US. Their business Sixth Sense Solutions offers people a great free dowsing website, www.discoveringdowsing.com, where you can buy their amazing Discovering Dowsing Course on DVD or thumb drive. They are authors of many books on dowsing and related topics that can be seen at Sixth Sense Books, www.sixthsensebooks.com.

For further information on dowsing
discoveringdowsing.com